4/40

GETTING MARRIED
*Looking forward to your wedding
and your life together*

JOANNA MOORHEAD was brought up in Manchester and Yorkshire, and since leaving university has worked as a journalist and writer in London. She is deputy editor of the *Catholic Herald*. She married in 1988.

Overcoming Common Problems Series

For a full list of titles please contact
Sheldon Press, Marylebone Road, London NW1 4DU

Beating Job Burnout
DR DONALD SCOTT

Beating the Blues
SUSAN TANNER AND JILLIAN
BALL

Being the Boss
STEPHEN FITZSIMON

Birth Over Thirty
SHEILA KITZINGER

Body Language
How to read others' thoughts by their
gestures
ALLAN PEASE

Bodypower
DR VERNON COLEMAN

Bodysense
DR VERNON COLEMAN

Calm Down
How to cope with frustration and anger
DR PAUL HAUCK

Changing Course
How to take charge of your career
SUE DYSON AND STEPHEN HOARE

Comfort for Depression
JANET HORWOOD

Complete Public Speaker
GYLES BRANDRETH

**Coping Successfully with Your Child's
Asthma**
DR PAUL CARSON

**Coping Successfully with Your Hyperactive
Child**
DR PAUL CARSON

**Coping Successfully with Your Irritable
Bowel**
ROSEMARY NICOL

Coping with Anxiety and Depression
SHIRLEY TRICKETT

Coping with Blushing
DR ROBERT EDELMANN

Coping with Cot Death
SARAH MURPHY

Coping with Depression and Elation
DR PATRICK McKEON

Coping with Stress
DR GEORGIA WITKIN-LANOIL

Coping with Suicide
DR DONALD SCOTT

Coping with Thrush
CAROLINE CLAYTON

Curing Arthritis – The Drug-Free Way
MARGARET HILLS

Curing Arthritis Diet Book
MARGARET HILLS

**Curing Coughs, Colds and Flu – The
Drug-Free Way**
MARGARET HILLS

Curing Illness – The Drug-Free Way
MARGARET HILLS

Depression
DR PAUL HAUCK

Divorce and Separation
ANGELA WILLANS

Don't Blame Me!
How to stop blaming yourself
and other people
TONY GOUGH

The Epilepsy Handbook
SHELAGH McGOVERN

**Everything You Need to Know about
Adoption**
MAGGIE JONES

**Everything You Need to Know about
Contact Lenses**
DR ROBERT YOUNGSON

**Everything You Need to Know about
Osteoporosis**
ROSEMARY NICOL

Overcoming Common Problems Series

Everything You Need to Know about Shingles
DR ROBERT YOUNGSON

Everything You Need to Know about Your Eyes
DR ROBERT YOUNGSON

Family First Aid and Emergency Handbook
DR ANDREW STANWAY

Feverfew
A traditional herbal remedy for migraine and arthritis
DR STEWART JOHNSON

Fight Your Phobia and Win
DAVID LEWIS

Getting Along with People
DIANNE DOUBTFIRE

Getting Married
JOANNA MOORHEAD

Goodbye Backache
DR DAVID IMRIE WITH COLLEEN DIMSON

Heart Attacks – Prevent and Survive
DR TOM SMITH

Helping Children Cope with Divorce
ROSEMARY WELLS

Helping Children Cope with Grief
ROSEMARY WELLS

Helping Children Cope with Stress
URSULA MARKHAM

Hold Your Head Up High
DR PAUL HAUCK

How to be a Successful Secretary
SUE DYSON AND STEPHEN HOARE

How to Be Your Own Best Friend
DR PAUL HAUCK

How to Control your Drinking
DRS W. MILLER AND R. MUNOZ

How to Cope with Stress
DR PETER TYRER

How to Cope with Tinnitus and Hearing Loss
DR ROBERT YOUNGSON

How to Cope with Your Child's Allergies
DR PAUL CARSON

How to Cure Your Ulcer
ANNE CHARLISH AND DR BRIAN GAZZARD

How to Do What You Want to Do
DR PAUL HAUCK

How to Get Things Done
ALISON HARDINGHAM

How to Improve Your Confidence
DR KENNETH HAMBLY

How to Interview and Be Interviewed
MICHELE BROWN AND GYLES BRANDRETH

How to Love a Difficult Man
NANCY GOOD

How to Love and be Loved
DR PAUL HAUCK

How to Make Successful Decisions
ALISON HARDINGHAM

How to Move House Successfully
ANNE CHARLISH

How to Pass Your Driving Test
DONALD RIDLAND

How to Say No to Alcohol
KEITH McNEILL

How to Spot Your Child's Potential
CECILE DROUIN AND ALAIN DUBOS

How to Stand up for Yourself
DR PAUL HAUCK

How to Start a Conversation and Make Friends
DON GABOR

How to Stop Smoking
GEORGE TARGET

How to Stop Taking Tranquillisers
DR PETER TYRER

How to Stop Worrying
DR FRANK TALLIS

How to Study Successfully
MICHELE BROWN

Overcoming Common Problems Series

Hysterectomy
SUZIE HAYMAN

Jealousy
DR PAUL HAUCK

Learning from Experience
A woman's guide to getting
older without panic
PATRICIA O'BRIEN

Learning to Live with Multiple Sclerosis
DR ROBERT POVEY, ROBIN DOWIE
AND GILLIAN PRETT

Living Alone – A Woman's Guide
LIZ McNEILL TAYLOR

Living Through Personal Crisis
ANN KAISER STEARNS

Living with Grief
DR TONY LAKE

Living with High Blood Pressure
DR TOM SMITH

Loneliness
DR TONY LAKE

Making Marriage Work
DR PAUL HAUCK

Making the Most of Loving
GILL COX AND SHEILA DAINOW

Making the Most of Yourself
GILL COX AND SHEILA DAINOW

Managing Two Careers
How to survive as a working mother
PATRICIA O'BRIEN

Meeting People is Fun
How to overcome shyness
DR PHYLLIS SHAW

Menopause
RAEWYN MACKENZIE

The Nervous Person's Companion
DR KENNETH HAMBLY

Overcoming Fears and Phobias
DR TONY WHITEHEAD

Overcoming Shyness
A woman's guide
DIANNE DOUBTFIRE

Overcoming Stress
DR VERNON COLEMAN

Overcoming Tension
DR KENNETH HAMBLY

Overcoming Your Nerves
DR TONY LAKE

The Parkinson's Disease Handbook
DR RICHARD GODWIN-AUSTEN

Say When!
Everything a woman needs to know about
alcohol and drinking problems
ROSEMARY KENT

Self-Help for your Arthritis
EDNA PEMBLE

Slay Your Own Dragons
How women can overcome
self-sabotage in love and work
NANCY GOOD

Sleep Like a Dream – The Drug-Free Way
ROSEMARY NICOL

Solving your Personal Problems
PETER HONEY

A Special Child in the Family
Living with your sick or disabled child
DIANA KIMPTON

Think Your Way to Happiness
DR WINDY DRYDEN AND JACK GORDON

Trying to Have a Baby?
Overcoming infertility and child loss
MAGGIE JONES

Why Be Afraid?
How to overcome your fears
DR PAUL HAUCK

Women and Depression
A practical self-help guide
DEIDRE SANDERS

You and Your Varicose Veins
DR PATRICIA GILBERT

Your Arthritic Hip and You
GEORGE TARGET

Your Grandchild and You
ROSEMARY WELLS

Overcoming Common Problems

GETTING MARRIED

*Looking forward to your wedding
and your life together*

Joanna Moorhead

SHELDON PRESS
LONDON

First published in Great Britain in 1991
Sheldon Press, SPCK, Marylebone Road, London NW1 4DU

British Library Cataloguing in Publication Data
Moorhead, Joanna
Getting married: preparing for your life together.
1. Marriage
I. Title
306.81

ISBN 0–85969–622–7

Photoset by Deltatype Ltd, Ellesmere Port, Cheshire
Printed in Great Britain by Courier International Ltd, Tiptree, Essex

Contents

	Introduction	1
1	The Proposal	5
2	Whys and Wherefores	19
3	A Religious Wedding	29
4	The Civil Service	44
5	Memories to Treasure	58
6	A Feast of Ideas	64
7	All Dressed Up	78
8	The Price of Love	87
9	Ever After	97
	Index	109

Introduction

When I got engaged four years ago I was, like many brides-to-be, fairly ignorant about the business of getting married. Keen to find out what was involved, I headed off to my local bookshop, hoping to find some helpful volume to guide me through the plans and preparations and give me a few ideas about the possibilities.

The words of wisdom on offer horrified me. Most were contained in books called things like 'Wedding Etiquette' and 'How to Plan the Perfect Wedding', and consisted of pages and pages of non-negotiable rules and regulations determining everything from the advisable month to wed to the colour of the carnation to be worn by the best man. Nothing, it seemed, came down to personal preference or was geared to reflect the life I and my partner lived; the main aim at a wedding, it transpired, was to follow to the letter a Victorian code of formality and to diverge from the norm as little as possible.

It seemed extraordinary to me then, and it seems even more bizarre to me now, that we should have believed these defenders of wedding day etiquette for so long. What, after all, can be the point of allowing ourselves to be submerged beneath a machinery which has virtually no relevance to the lives most of us lead today? Why should we subject ourselves to a dictated set of rules when our wedding day could be a more meaningful celebration of the two individuals who have decided to spend the rest of their lives together?

All this is not, however, tantamount to rejecting tradition, which I think can make a valuable and useful contribution at a wedding. Tradition binds us to the past, and means that in our wedding there can be an echo of the wedding of our parents and grandparents; it also serves to remind us that the institution we are entering into is an old-established one. But tradition should enhance our wedding, not create it; our ideas

1

about marriage come partly from the past, but they come partly from ourselves, too, and from the philosophy and ideas of our own time, and these elements ought also to be represented at a wedding.

Some people worry that if they try to introduce their own ideas they will scandalize their guests, who will spend the whole time muttering about the shortcomings of the occasion. In reality, however, it seems that almost exactly the opposite applies: guests, especially those who frequent rather a lot of weddings or who have frequented rather a lot in their time, love something different. They also remember something different, not only the week after but a year, even a decade or several decades, on. It is one of the great ironies of wedding days that couples and their parents strive for months to achieve perfection, and then it is the imperfect elements, the bits that go wrong, which so often inject a bit of character and style into the day.

Planning a wedding which reflects yourselves and your relationship has the advantage, too, of giving you and your partner time and opportunity to sit down together and talk through what really matters to you both. Too often the months of an engagement are a time when a relationship is 'on ice': the demands of trying to follow the etiquette book to the letter allow little time for the couple at the centre of the wedding to plan their lives when the honeymoon is over. But talking about the kind of choices and possibilities a wedding day affords will inevitably, I believe, lead a couple to make discoveries about what matters and is important to each other, and about what is important in their life together. For example, talking about who to invite to the wedding will help you understand who is important in your partner's life, and will help you communicate to him who is important in yours. Talking about the finances of the wedding may reveal your attitude to and worries about money.

It is worth being aware of the insights you can gain into yourself, your partner and your relationship through planning your wedding. Many of the decisions you must make give you a chance to talk about things which are important to both of you. Take advantage of these opportunities to enrich your relationship and find out more about one another. Often, just talking through what you are planning and hoping for from your wedding will raise useful topics. And you may find it helpful to read through the 'talking points' at the end of each chapter of this book, which may give you an outline of the sorts of areas you might like to discuss with your partner. Don't feel these points are exercises which you should set time aside to do in a very formal way: they are intended, rather, as pointers, ideas you might like to use. Not all of them will be relevant to you and your partner: but you find some of them spark off a useful conversation.

This book, then, is not a blueprint for a perfect wedding, nor is it a catalogue of rules which brides and bridegrooms must follow to the letter. It is, rather, a collection of ideas and possibilities, many illustrated by the real-life experiences of the recently-married couples I have spoken to, which you might like to think about using or adapting on your wedding day. It is, I hope, a book which will inspire rather than straitjacket its readers, giving them the confidence to inject at least a little of themselves into a day which should be one of the most meaningful of their lives.

Many people have given of their time, ideas and energy to help put this book together. I would like to thank, in particular, the couples who so generously shared with me the stories of their own wedding days, and allowed me to quote their experiences. The advice and guidance of the following was also invaluable: Jeffrey Brumenfeld of the Jewish Marriage Council; Canon Peter Chambers of the Church of England; Fr John Guest of the Roman Catholic Church; Sue Tuckwell of Relate in Bristol, Roger Lewis of the General Register Office in London, and Penny Mansfield of One Plus One. I am extremely grateful, too, to Jean Judge and Margaret Grimer of the Catholic Marriage Advisory Council for their support and advice at the start of this project, and for permission to include in this book the quiz 'What is important to you?' Thanks, also, to my family and friends, particularly Peter Stanford, for their helpful comments; and to Gary

INTRODUCTION

Smith, my husband, for his love and support and, perhaps most of all, his word processor.

1

The Proposal

Will you marry me? It's a question that's been written in the sky, broadcast over the airwaves, telexed across the world. One French chef is said to have written his proposal on a bit of rice paper which he stuffed into a chicken dish to be served to the woman he loved when she came to dine at his restaurant, while Prince Aya, second son of Emperor Akihito of Japan, was reported to have asked Princess Kiko to marry him while the two stood waiting for the traffic lights to change on a street corner in Tokyo. Parachutist Corporal Stephen Apps slipped a ring on the finger of his beloved, Caroline Wallace, as the two hurtled towards the ground from 12,000 feet, while holiday-maker Trevor Sansome was even higher in the sky when he popped the question to his girlfriend Tracy Lennon in October 1990: he asked the pilot on their charter flight to Greece to make his request over the intercom. The pilot agreed, and amused fellow-travellers heard the announcement: 'We're flying at 29,000 feet – and by the way, Tracy, will you marry Trevor?'

But for all the publicity a few proposals have received the vast majority remain, for all time, an intensely personal memory. Once two people have agreed that marriage is their chosen course, the world is naturally informed . . . but many couples choose never to share the details of that most private of moments, the exchange which led them to the altar.

Traditionally, it's always been the man who's done the asking, although a survey in 1989 found that only 11 per cent of men had proposed by going down on one knee and begging for their beloved's hand. Women, of course, have supposedly only had leave to do the asking in a leap year, although women from Scarlett O'Hara in *Gone With The Wind* to Lady Caroline Lamb have turned convention on its head and asked their men to marry them. So too did Queen Victoria, urged on no doubt by royal protocol, when in 1839 she asked her 'beloved Albert' for his hand.

At about ½ p 12 I sent for Albert; he came to the Closet where I was alone, and after a few minutes I said to him, that I thought he must be aware why I wished (him) to come here, and that it would make me too happy if he would consent to what I wished (to marry me); we embraced each other over and over again, and he was so kind, so affectionate; . . . I told him I was quite unworthy of him and kissed his dear hand – he said he would be very happy (to marry me) and was so kind and seemed so happy, that I really felt it was the happiest brightest moment in my life. . . .

Queen Victoria, from her Journal for 15 October 1839

Many proposals today are just as romantic.

It was Christmas Day, and we were staying in a cottage in the Lake District with my parents. Simon hadn't got me a present, but said he'd buy me something when we went back to London. It seems really obvious, looking back, what was going to happen, but somehow I didn't cotton on and that made it all the more romantic. All afternoon he kept saying we should go for a walk, just the two of us, but of course it poured down all day. In the end, at about 4.00 pm and just as it was getting dark, he persuaded me to go out in the car for a drive. We went down to the lakeside – it was all completely deserted, as it was such a horrible day – and he somehow got me to get out of the car. We went and stood by the water's edge watching the rain fall and suddenly he grabbed my hand and just said it . . . I said yes straight away, the tears falling down my cheeks. I got a terrible cold the following week, after standing about in the rain for so long!

Anna, 28, a teacher; married to Simon for 18 months

Judging by the 'forthcoming marriages' sections of the national daily newspapers, many proposals take place, as Simon's did, on a 'special' day, such as St Valentine's Day, Christmas Day or New Year. Others happen on a date significant for the couple alone – one partner's birthday, perhaps, or the anniversary of a first meeting or first date.

But not all couples have a formal request-and-acceptance proposal like Simon and Anna's; for some, the decision to marry is more of a kind of general dawning that this is the way both want things to turn out.

> Jeremy certainly never asked me to marry him . . . it wouldn't have fitted in with the way we run our relationship. I think what happened was that we very gradually, over a long time, just came to realize it was what we both wanted. We talked about the future, obviously, and it became clear that we both saw the other as playing a continuing role in the future. I don't remember a day when we suddenly said 'we're getting married'. It just crept in over time, a sort of unspoken understanding that it was what we would one day do.
>
> *Alice, 25, an artist; married to social worker*
> *Jeremy for 3 months*

Why get married at all?

In the past, the decision to get married signalled a fairly definite threshold in the lives of two people. It marked the beginning of a relationship which would blossom and grow, hopefully, during many happy years together. Although the couple were likely to know each other to a certain extent, the basis of their knowledge of one another would probably have been gleaned from going out together rather than staying in together, and so would have been limited to socializing with one another in public places. Indeed, there have been certain points in history – the more prudish years of the Victorian era, for example – when nicely-brought up girls were never left alone with their suitors, so a couple would have to do all their courting within sight, if not earshot, of others. And even as recently as 30 years ago, private moments would have been fairly rare occasions for some young couples.

Contrast all this with today, when a growing number of

people – as many as one in two couples – live together before they even think about whether to marry, and it quickly becomes clear that the attractions marriage held for our parents – privacy, a home of their own, the chance to get down to some real sex – are very different from the factors which lead so many of us to choose it today.

So what is the magical ingredient which motivates us into marriage today? Why, in this age of living together and with sex almost *de rigeur* before you even think about waltzing up the aisle, do we do it?

For most of the couples I interviewed in the course of researching this book, the single most important factor was the anticipated arrival of children. A minority were actually expecting a baby at the time of their wedding, while the majority had already begun to think about the possibility of starting a family and wanted to create a stable, secure 'nest' in which to raise their offspring. The fact that up to one in three marriages ends in divorce, with the figure still rising, and that each year many hundreds of thousands of children witness the break-up of their parents' union, seemed not to deter them. Whatever the hard facts, the image of being able to create a happy, bonded, legally-recognized family still clearly has a strong pull.

Often in conjunction with children, many couples cited reasons such as 'parental pressure' or even peer pressure as a contributory factor in the decision to wed. The combination of marriage as both highly pleasing to most parents and firmly fashionable among friends (marriage today is as popular as it was at the start of the 1980s) often provides a tug too strong for even the most reluctant bride and groom to resist. And one marriage can often, quite literally, lead to another; my husband and I can't be the only ones who began to plan our nuptials while sipping champagne at the wedding reception of close friends.

And then there are all those difficult-to-put-into-words motives which many couples try to express to explain their decision to wed. It's all to do with a mysterious change of status – not merely a different status for the female partner, which many feminist-minded women would anyway want to reject – but a new status for you as a couple, a new set of expectations about what the two of you represent. As sociologist and marriage researcher Penny Mansfield puts it, if one member of an unmarried partnership takes on a new job and goes to live in New York, many friends might conclude that the relationship was over. But if one half of a married couple went to live in New York, people would certainly not take it as read that the marriage had come to an end. In exchanging vows, two people create an almost tangible bond which is separate from, though hopefully intertwined with, their relationship. So however strange or fragile or unconventional their life with one another becomes in the future, they remain married, and outsiders will continue to consider them a couple until some formal announcement is made to the contrary.

Even being engaged usually means people will treat you differently as a couple. Indeed, for some couples this is a factor in deciding to become betrothed in the first place.

I was 18 and Brian was 20 when we decided to get engaged. We'd been going out together for a few months, and it just seemed the right thing to do. We were quite sure we were right for one another. Also, being engaged meant my mum let us live together in her flat at weekends while she went to stay with my grandmother, so it gave us a chance to develop our relationship, to spend more time together and become closer.

Karen, 24, a computer programmer; married to Brian for three years. The couple live outside Manchester

What does marriage really mean?

It sounds straightforward enough, doesn't it? The pair of you go along to a church or register office, probably surrounded by family and friends, exchange your vows and have a party and that's it – you're married. But does everyone understand the same thing by the term 'getting married'? Surprisingly enough, they don't. Marriage means quite different things to different people.

For Catholics, for example, marriage is a sacrament of the Church, and getting married is, for most Catholics, an important religious occasion. It is also a public declaration that the couple is willing to have children: they are asked to state during the ceremony that they have every intention of starting a family.

Roman Catholics are not alone in seeing marriage as being of religious significance, of course. Many people who believe in a God, Christian or otherwise, consider their marriage a fitting occasion to seek the blessing of the Almighty, and choose a ceremony at which God's name is invoked. Indeed, marriages solemnized according to religious rites account for just over half of all marriages in this country, and during the last decade the number of 'religious' weddings even increased slightly, from 49 to 52 per cent.

Of these marriages, the majority – around two-thirds – take place in Anglican churches. Another 14 per cent take place in Roman Catholic churches, and about 10 per cent in Methodist chapels; other denominations account for smaller slices of the wedding 'cake'. Around 1 in 20 religious wedding services are celebrated, not by Christians, but by Jews, Muslims, Sikhs, Hindus or Buddhists. Although many couples who marry according to these very varied rites probably do not give a great deal of thought to the religious element, there is no doubt that the majority attach some significance to the fact that God's blessing was invoked to seal their union.

> As soon as we decided to make a lifelong commitment to one another, we recognized that it involved a spiritual dimension. We were both brought up as Christians, so church was the obvious place to go. It means something to us that we made our vows before an altar.
>
> *Alice*

Priests and vicars report that often people become more committed to their faiths while they are preparing for marriage. It seems that some of us are particularly open, not surprisingly, to spiritual ideas around the time when we are taking such an important life-step.

This openness to spirituality is felt by non-believers as well as believers. Indeed, it is one of the reasons behind the increasing number of humanist marriage celebrations. Some people, especially those who feel register offices do not put enough meaning into the ceremony, opt for a humanist service in the hope of creating more of a sense of occasion within which to make their vows – without having to resort to the hypocrisy, as they see it, of a church wedding.

For others, of course, the register office provides all they need.

Getting married for the second time in a register office with minimal fuss and just a few friends there might seem to some to be much less of a rite of passage than a big white wedding in a church, which was the kind of do I'd had the first time around. But I certainly didn't feel any 'less married' because of it. Peter and I saw getting married as a private thing, really, a seal on our relationship. We were saying to one another that we were entirely serious about our commitment, that we really intended to spend the rest of our lives together. In a way, it seemed more of a commitment than it had the first time, because in the register office we were distilling it down to the essence, making our essential promise to one another the only important part of what we were doing. We weren't thinking of our wedding as a social event or something for other people, we were thinking of it in terms of what we meant to one another.

Angela, 28

But wherever it happens, marriage means two things: firstly, a personal commitment to one another, and secondly, a public acknowledgement of our intention to build, or more usually these days continue to build, a life together. The 'public' nature of marriage, the fact that couples make their vows before a minimum of three people and usually a whole lot more, is important in two respects, as both a declaration to the community at large, and a call to individuals within the community to witness the commitment being made.

Getting together a large bunch of friends and family before whom to swear undying love signifies great strength in a relationship, in that we as a couple feel brave and sure enough to stand up and declare our love. But, oddly, it also leaves us with a kind of vulnerability, in that we often feel that, having taken this one enormous leap in front of everyone we know, we must henceforward always present them with a united front. It's almost as though, having made our pledge, we feel we would reveal a chink in our armour if we were to admit some minor row or disagreement. It is often quite extraordinary how people who before marriage would happily report falling out and arguments to their friends transform into resolute non-complainers after the honeymoon. Which is fine, of course, if there really is nothing to complain about; but few of us go very long without some kind of disagreement, and sometimes it can help to discuss the issue with a third party. After all conflict, many psychologists and researchers believe, is the key to growth in a relationship.

Lastly, marriage has meaning – of course – in a legal sense. While married, and whatever else may happen, we cannot marry another person; so in the eyes of the law at least, we are monogamous. Married couples are also expected to have sex with one another; indeed, the marriage is not deemed complete until the couple have consummated it. And any children born to a married couple are presumed in law to be fathered by the husband, and are considered 'legitimate'. Both halves of a married couple also have rights over a shared home (unlike unmarried couples) and are also entitled to the married couple's tax allowance.

A statement of intent

There's nothing nicer than being the bearer of glad tidings –

and what could be gladder than the news that you and your beloved are to wed?

Who, though, should be the first to hear your good news? In the old days, when prospective husbands were expected to ask her father for their intended's hand, the etiquette was much more rigid: the bride's parents would inevitably be the first to know, followed by the bridegroom's, both families, close friends, and then (usually via a press announcement) wider acquaintances, business associates and distant kin. Today the form of who to tell first is more blurred, although the vast majority of people still want their parents to know before anyone else.

After that, the order of telling is more or less up to you, although you should bear in mind that old relatives and friends may take offence at hearing the news from someone other than yourselves. Similarly, if you're putting a notice in a newspaper you should ensure it doesn't appear until you've given the news to anyone who should hear it direct.

Traditionally, well-heeled couples announced their engagements in the 'forthcoming marriages' section of a national newspaper – preferably *The Times*. But that was in the days when newspaper readership was more homogenous; today, few of us can boast an entire set of friends who read one newspaper exclusively – and inserting a notice in each of the quality broadsheets will set you back several hundred pounds.

Better value for money comes in the shape of your local rag, which will charge you considerably less per column line and probably provide you with more chance of spreading your news to people you know, rather than just paying to inform the browsers and social climbers who go through the 'court pages' with a fine-tooth comb. But whether you opt to publish your engagement in a local or national paper or both, be prepared to provide what you want to say in writing, usually accompanied by the signatures of both of those involved.

How you word your announcement is often determined not by your personal choice but by the individual style of the paper concerned, as some newspapers insist on the same phrasing for each notice. The most usual format, favoured by the nationals and many locals, is as follows:

Mr John Smith and Miss Jenny Brown

The engagement is announced between John Andrew, elder son of Mr and Mrs Malcolm Smith, of Uckfield, Sussex, and Jenny Sarah, only daughter of Sqn Ldr and Mrs Simon Brown, of Peterborough, Cambridgeshire.

These days fewer and fewer families follow the neat pattern of both sets of parents still being attached to one another, so if necessary describe yourself as 'only daughter of Sqn Ldr Simon Brown of Peterborough, Cambridgeshire and Mrs Maureen Winter of Bath', or whatever.

What papers may be less able to cater for, unfortunately, are personal preferences about the way engagements are worded. For example, you may wish to break with tradition and name the female partner of the union first, both in the heading and in the text, although some papers will, alas, tell you this is 'not our usual style' and therefore unacceptable. Or you might want to dispense altogether with your parents' names, particularly if they are not especially involved in the preparations for the marriage. Some papers, including the otherwise ultratraditionalist Daily Telegraph, will allow this; but The Telegraph would be unlikely to look favourably on publishing the following sort of announcement, should you prefer it:

Jenny Brown of London SW4 and John Smith of Richmond, Surrey, would like to announce that they have decided to spend the rest of their lives together, and that their marriage will take place early next year.

Newspapers such as The Independent and The Times, on the other hand, would be willing to consider an 'unorthodox' announcement, although the couple's full names will normally be required to go at the start of the notice, and The

Times is likely to insist on the man's name preceding that of his bride-to-be, a convention which some couples consider to be unfair and outdated.

Choosing a ring

Some avant garde couples these days eschew the tradition of buying the bride-to-be a ring to mark the engagement. This may be to do with the fact that there's no male equivalent, so some women tend to feel that wearing a sparkling stone on their left hand means only one thing, and that's 'get off, she's mine'. Interestingly, though, the tradition of wearing wedding, as opposed to engagement, rings has meanwhile increased. In Britain, even if not in the rest of Europe, the usual thing has always been for the female half of the partnership to be given a gold or platinum band during the wedding ceremony, but these days large numbers of bride-grooms – as many as 30 per cent – are receiving them too. Many people believe, mistakenly, that the exchanging of rings is an essential part of the wedding ceremony, which may also explain why the tradition has remained so strong.

The vast majority of people, though, don't think twice about whether or not to make the most of the excuse to buy the bride-to-be an attractive, and usually valuable, piece of jewellery. An engagement ring is certainly a major purchase, and worth taking some time and trouble over.

Diamonds – perhaps because they represent the hardest substance known, perhaps because the Greeks believed they reflected the constant flame of love – have traditionally been *the* stone for an engagement ring. In the past a single 'solitaire' diamond was the only possible choice for a bride-to-be's finger, but these days many couples opt for a coloured stone – a sapphire, perhaps, or a ruby, surrounded by smaller diamonds. Both the Princess of Wales and the Duchess of York have engagement rings in this style, setting the trend for a million look-alikes. Other people prefer to be completely original in their choice of engagement ring – former astronaut

Edwin 'Buzz' Aldrin had a lunar stone collected on his 1969 space mission made into an engagement ring for his intended.

Whatever kind of ring you're looking for, the best advice is to go to a reputable jeweller, ask his or her advice, and make sure you are completely happy about your choice before you actually commit yourself. You might want to come back and try the ring you like another day, when you might be in a different mood, rather than making such an important decision in one go. And it's very important to think about what kind of wedding ring you'll eventually buy before you get your engagement ring. Otherwise you could end up – as I did – finding the platinum wedding ring you'd set your heart on is completely impractical with an 18-carat gold engagement ring, as the harder platinum rubs away the softer gold if the two are in constant contact.

Platinum, a purer metal than gold and quite a lot more expensive, is worth considering as a possibility for both the engagement and wedding rings as it wears much more slowly, especially if you're keen on a wedding ring with an engraved pattern. But gold remains the favourite, as it has done ever since the ancient Egyptians first thought of incorporating it in their wedding rings. Indeed, it was the Egyptians who began the practice of wearing wedding rings at all, placing them on the third finger of the left hand in the belief that a vein from there ran directly to the heart. The ring itself was significant too, in that it was unbroken and therefore symbolized the eternal nature of the relationship.

Most of the gold you'll find in jewellers' shops in Britain was mined in South Africa, and some couples prefer not to buy a commodity they believe still represents an immoral political system. One couple I spoke to had resolved not to have gold wedding rings as a result and bought silver bands instead. Yet it is possible to support gold producers nearer to home when you buy your rings – there is a Welsh gold mining industry, and Royal wedding rings are usually made from Welsh gold. It costs more than the South African equivalent and is hallmarked with a distinctive sack of gold. Another possibility is to buy a Nicaraguan gold ring – some 'alternative', fair trade organizations market these in Britain.

Gold engagement and wedding rings, wherever their metal originated, are usually either nine carat (37.5 per cent pure gold) or 18 carat (75 per cent pure gold). Twenty-four carat, or pure gold, is usually considered too soft to stand up to the wear and tear. The colour of the gold depends on the other metals which have been mixed with it: copper gives a pink or bronze tinge, while white gold contains nickel.

It's probably a good idea to be fairly conservative in your choice of wedding band, as you are likely to wear it more often than your engagement ring. Some women dislike ever having to remove their wedding rings, so they should be practical as well as pretty. And don't dismiss the idea of a plain gold band –they're still the most popular, and enduring, style.

Talking Points

● Write down the important dates in your relationship – the days or perhaps the periods which you believe marked a turning-point in your relationship. Ask your partner to do the same. Then compare notes. Which one of you realized first that the other might be a lifelong partner? What prompted the realization? Share your memories together.

● Does anything about marriage frighten you? If so, is the fear based on someone else's experience (e.g., what happened to your best friend when she got married), or does it reveal something about yourself? Whatever you fear and for whatever reason you fear it, tell your partner your worries and ask him about his. Communicating well is the key to a good relationship, and that means letting your partner know the things that worry you as well as those that make you happy.

● Celebrate your love by telling each other what you most value about his or her character. Describe a time when this trait was most clearly evident, and tell your partner how much you loved/admired/cared for him at that moment. Keep in mind, now and in the future, all the good things about your partner which led you to choose him. Marriage Counsellors say that couples whose relationships are on the rocks have often forgotten what it was that made them first fall in love; when they remind themselves, they can often re-kindle the flame of their marriage.

2

Whys and Wherefores

When's it going to be?

As soon as you tell anyone that you've decided to get married, the first question they're likely to ask (after offering their congratulations, if you're lucky) is, 'When's it going to be?' Everyone you know, it seems, is suddenly keen to note the date down in their diaries in the hope that an invitation will be popping through their letter box.

As far as your party-loving friends are concerned, your wedding probably won't be able to happen soon enough. But don't let their enthusiasm for a good time push you into getting married a moment before you feel you're ready for it. Although some couples seem to work out all the details on the same evening they decide to get engaged, others very definitely prefer to wait – sometimes for quite a long time. There's no 'correct' length of time for an engagement to last.

We were engaged for 18 months which, looking back, seems an awfully long time. Some people more or less told me it was much too long at the time – one so-called friend even told me that the longer the engagement, the less likely it was that the marriage would last! But I felt a bit panicky about getting married – not because I was worried I was marrying the wrong person, but because I was afraid of giving up my independence – and I wanted to feel completely comfortable with it before I went ahead.

Anna

All the same, it is worth realizing that you'll probably have to plan your wedding day some time in advance, so naming a date isn't necessarily going to mean committing yourself to marriage in the very near future. Summer nuptials in particular are often tricky to plan, given their popularity. Saturdays in June, July and August are often booked up a year or more in advance, and couples determined to exchange their vows in these months may have to consider getting married on a Friday or Monday. More and more couples, in fact, are choosing days other than Saturdays for their weddings, having discovered that even if you find a caterer who's available for the August weekend you wanted, the chances are that the vicar is already going to be booked up. And if you're going for a register office wedding, synchronizing the different elements of ceremony and catering are made particularly tricky by the fact that you're unable to book the registrar more than three months in advance. To make matters easier for yourself, as well as bearing in mind the possibility of a weekday wedding, why not consider going for a day in September, when the weather can be warm and mellow, or even early October, which can be quite beautiful? Autumn weddings also give a whole wealth of opportunities for different flowers and rich colour schemes.

Don't rule out the early months of the year either. April and May can bring prolonged spells of warmth and sunshine, often better than the notoriously fickle weather of July. And don't be put off, if you're attracted to the idea of a May wedding, by that old saying that you'll 'rue the day'. Apart from being quite obviously inspired only by its rhyming potential, the adage is balanced by an ancient belief that as May was the month of the Virgin Mary, her special blessings would be showered on those who wed at that time.

Women who plan their wedding days more than three or four months in advance often worry about where the date will fall in their menstrual cycle. Unfortunately, particularly for those of us whose cycles are not as regular as clockwork, there has to be an element of luck as far as avoiding PMT or first-day cramps is concerned, so the best advice is probably to try to work out what stage of the month you're likely to be at and, having hopefully avoided a week when your period will be due, to forget all about it.

Even if, as the day nears, you realize your period might start on or around your wedding day, it's worth remembering that the nervousness and anxiety which inevitably accompanies the last few weeks and days before a wedding may well make your period late. If you're worried about being bloated or having tender breasts, you might consider taking diuretics, evening primrose oil or vitamin B6; talk to the doctor at your local well woman clinic for more advice. Alternatively, if you take the contraceptive pill and fear your period will start on or around your wedding day, you might like to talk to your doctor about the possibility of delaying it by taking one packet of pills immediately after another; with some brands of the drug, and provided you are relatively young, this can be quite safe.

As well as booking the church or register office and caterer, another thing to check on when organizing the date is that, as far as it's possible to anticipate, there won't be any traffic hold-ups in your area on the day you're going for. Obviously there's no way you can guard against motorway hold-ups slowing your guests down on their way to the ceremony, but you can check that there are no popular big events in your area set to clash with yours. Make sure, for example, that the local village or town isn't holding its annual gala or fête, and that any football ground or racecourse isn't planning a big match or meeting.

What kind of ceremony?

Another important decision you'll have to think about fairly early on is whether you want to get married in a church or at a register office. For some couples, of course, the question needs no discussion at all: if you're both devout Catholics, or practising Jews, you will simply head off to see the parish priest or local rabbi. But what do you do if you're a committed Christian and your partner is an equally sincere atheist who had hoped never to see the inside of a church again? Or if neither of you worships on a regular basis but you share some lukewarm belief about God probably being up there some-where? And again, how will you cope if you both feel you'd be happier with a civil ceremony but know your church-going mothers will be devastated if God doesn't feature at your nuptials?

Unfortunately, there are no straightforward answers to these tricky problems. The only solution is to work through them, to discuss them fully with your partner, and to arrive at a decision (often a compromise) which both of you feel comfortable with. Don't try to shirk the question of where you really want to get married by being talked into something without considering your own feelings on it, and don't allow anyone to pressurize or rush you into a decision. Spiritual beliefs, whether allied to an organized religion or of a more general kind, are important in a marriage. It's essential that you know and respect one another's views on what life is all about, even if you don't share the same opinions exactly (and which two human beings do?). Also, failing to get to grips with your partner's beliefs on God, religion, and the meaning of life now will only lead to bigger problems later on if and when you have children, as even the most deeply buried religious views, prejudices and ideas tend to come tearing to the surface when you come round to discuss what you're going to tell your own offspring.

There are no clear-cut questions which you should ask yourselves if you're unsure whether or not to opt for a church wedding (assuming, that is, that you're eligible for one anyway – for more information on this, see Chapter 3), but you should certainly ask yourselves whether either of you actually believes in God, even if it's just a feeling that somewhere, somehow, there's something bigger and better than us. Also, ask yourselves whether either of you attaches any value at all to the idea of getting married in the sight of God, in his house, and in his name. If the honest answer to either of these questions is no, you should think seriously about opting for a civil wedding. If you're very keen to have a traditional service, or want something more personal and meaningful than a standard register office do, why not consider a humanist ceremony? See Chapter 4 for more details on this.

You might also want to talk about how the one (or both) of you who doesn't hold strong beliefs in God is going to feel about walking up a church aisle to get married. Many people are afraid of feeling hypocritical about 'using' a church for their wedding when they wouldn't normally darken its doors. If you share this sense of unease, think carefully about what it means. If one of you is fairly religious and the other not at all, you might want to think about injecting a secular element into a religious service to reflect both your points of view – see Chapter 3 for further ideas on this.

Couples sometimes worry about whether it is wrong or inadvisable to get married in a church because they have been sharing their home or their bed before entering into matrimony. Although it's true that most religions frown upon pre-marital sex, more and more ministers of all faiths are turning a blind eye to it, and most are simply pleased that so many couples still see the church as a place to come at such an important time in life. As any sensible priest or vicar should realize, couples seeking marriage provide the Church with a unique opportunity to demonstrate its Christian warmth and welcome which, if properly dispensed, could in turn lead them to seek it out again in the future. So don't let fears of incurring the vicar's disapproval deter you from a church wedding.

Once you've arrived at a decision about what kind of ceremony to have, be prepared to explain to your families – together, if at all possible – the factors which influenced your choice. It's extremely important to be honest about your reasons and united in your resolve, especially if you're opting for something a bit unexpected (a register office ceremony despite coming from staunchly religious backgrounds, perhaps) or out of the ordinary (a humanist ceremony, for example). You must follow your own convictions rather than please your parents, but equally you owe them a full explanation of why you're planning it as you are. As well as being the only fair way to proceed, you will find that even where your family is upset or disappointed about your choice, they will at least respect your choice if you explain it.

Legal requirements

However small or informal a wedding you'd like to have, however little you care about etiquette or doing things properly, if you want to be married in the eyes of the law there are certain formalities you must go through. These formalities fall into two major categories: those which apply if you're planning a Church of England service, and those which apply if you're planning any other kind of ceremony in either a place of worship or a register office. The difference in procedure is due to the fact that the Anglican Church, being the established denomination in the country, has its own system which fulfils all the legal requirements.

If you're opting for marriage in the Church of England, then, the most usual course of action is for banns to be read out in the parish where your ceremony is to be held plus the parish or parishes where you live, if these are different. The banns are read out on three successive Sundays, and once they have been called the wedding must take place within three months.

Marriage after banns is usually the cheapest option if you choose an Anglican church wedding, but the necessity of calling them can be dispensed with if the second possibility, marriage by common licence, is considered more suitable. You might be advised to marry by common licence for a variety of reasons: sometimes it is for a practical reason as in, for example, the fact that a wedding by licence can take place more quickly, while other times the Church advises a licence to be issued as when, for example, a British subject is marrying a foreigner.

Whatever the reason for it, the marriage by common licence requires one party to swear that there is no legal impediment to the marriage and that both members of the partnership consent to it going ahead. He or she is also required to confirm that one or both members of the couple have lived in the parish for at least 15 days before the date of the application to marry.

Superintendent Registrar's Certificates can also be issued for Church of England weddings but this is quite unusual. It may be deemed appropriate, however, in cases where one partner has been divorced, or where the couple are elderly and want a quiet wedding without banns.

For those getting married at anything other than a Church of England service (i.e. for register office weddings or weddings conducted according to the rites of any other denomination), the Superintendent Registrar's Certificate is the usual form of permission. To obtain a certificate, you must first give notice of your intention to marry. If you both live in the same registration district and intend to get married in that district, only one of you needs to go to the register office to give notice. However, if you live in different districts or intend to get married in another district – for example, if you both live in the same house in London but wish to marry in the bride's parents' home town of Bristol – you must each give notice, with one of you (usually it will be the bride) giving notice in the area where your wedding is to be held.

To satisfy the law exactly, you are required to live in the district for at least seven days before you give notice there. However, this so-called residence qualification is due to be scrapped under reforms which should be introduced within the next few years, and in practice many registrars turn a blind eye to accepting notice from someone they suspect does not really reside in the area. The qualification is widely recognized as a legacy of an era when women, in whose parishes marriages have traditionally taken place, tended to live in their parental homes until matrimony. These days, of course, the majority of women have lived independently prior to their marriage, often in a different part of the country, but the custom of getting wed from the bride's parents' home remains strong.

When you go to the register office to give notice, you will probably be asked to produce your birth certificate and that of your spouse-to-be, and/or some form of ID such as your passport. If you are marrying a foreigner, his or her passport will certainly be required. If either you or your partner has been married before, you will need to show the registrar divorce papers or a death certificate. In the case of all these documents, the official will not be able to accept photocopies.

The registrar will also ask, in best sexist tradition, for your father's name and occupation (although after the new reforms come into being, mothers' names and occupations are also to be included in the register entry). This, along with the details of your full name and date of birth and that of your partner, will be entered in the notice book. Twenty-one days after these details have been written down, the registrar can issue the certificate which will permit your marriage; once this has happened, you must marry within three months.

Marriage by certificate is the more common, and certainly the cheaper option, if you are getting married anywhere other than an Anglican church. However, if you want to get married in a hurry and don't have time to wait 21 days, there is another possibility: the Superintendent Registrar's certificate and licence, usually referred to simply as a 'licence'.

To obtain a licence, only one of the couple needs to give notice. Both of them must, however, be in England or Wales or usually live in England or Wales, and at least one of the two must have lived in the district for the last 15 days. One clear day later, other than a Sunday, Christmas Day or Good Friday, the licence for the marriage can be issued and is valid, as in the case of the certificate, for three months.

The only other sort of licence is that issued where one of the parties is too ill to be moved and the ceremony must take place at a hospital bedside. If the wedding is to be an Anglican one, the Archbishop of Canterbury can issue a licence allowing this; if a civil marriage or a marriage according to the rites of any other denominations is to be performed, the licence will be issued by the Registrar General.

This rather confusing system of certificates, licences, notice time and different procedures is to have a complete overhaul under the forthcoming change in legislation. However, if and when the new legislation on marriage comes into force, there is likely to be just one single system of giving notice of marriage, which will include a standard minimum waiting period of 15 days between giving notice and the marriage. Registrars will be given discretionary powers to reduce this period in what the Government White Paper referred to as 'exceptional circumstances'. In addition, the permission for a marriage to take place will no longer, as it does now, expire after three months; after the Act comes into force, couples will have six months to wed once the registrar's authority has been given.

Marriage in Scotland

The system of giving notice in Scotland is in many ways simpler than it is for England. Indeed, several of the changes proposed in the Government's 1990 White Paper are already usual practice over the border.

Each party is required to complete a form called a marriage notice which, along with a fee, must be given to the registrar responsible for the district in which you plan to wed. Officially, you are required to give a minimum of 15 days' notice, but registrars suggest you give your notice in at least a month before your chosen date, and six weeks if one or both of you has been married before.

Once the registrar is satisfied that all is in order, but not more than seven days before the wedding, the registrar will issue a document called a Marriage Schedule, which must be collected in person by you or your partner. The schedule must then be passed on to the person officiating at the ceremony, completed by those taking part on the day, and returned to the registrar within three days of the service. If you are having a civil ceremony, however, you will not be issued with the schedule, although it will be completed during the wedding in the same way.

Talking Points

● Tell your partner about why you believe in God or don't believe in God, or why you sometimes believe and sometimes don't. Ask your partner to listen to your arguments and feelings without interrupting, and if you feel he or she doesn't always understand your point of view on religion, tell him or her why this is. Afterwards, repeat the exercise with your partner telling you his or her feelings on religion. If you follow different religious traditions, talking openly about your faith and explaining it will help banish any erroneous ideas you or your partner may hold – most of us harbour prejudices about religions we don't belong to – and will also help your partner to understand where you stand as an individual.

● Think of something which really matters in your partner's life (it might be his or her religious belief, or a cultural interest), and tell him or her why you are impressed by it and why you think it matters to him or her. Then ask whether s/he agrees with your interpretation. This is another way in which you can 'show you care' for your partner and respect his views, as well as establishing how much you understand about something which is important to him.

● Talk together about your wedding service and what it will mean to you and to your relationship. Is it important to you that your family and friends will be there to hear you exchange your vows, or would the service be equally meaningful if just the two of you and a couple of witnesses were there? This discussion will make you both more aware of the importance each attaches to links with family and friends, as well as helping you work out what kind of service will suit you both.

Useful Addresses

General Register Office, St Catherine's House, 10 Kingsway, London WC2B 6JP

General Register Office, New Register House, Edinburgh, EH1 3YT

General Register Office, Oxford House, 49–55 Chichester Street, Belfast BT1 4HF

3

A Religious Wedding

For as long as human beings have been building churches, they've also been getting married in them. Today, despite the fact that fewer people than ever before actually go to church to worship on a regular basis, the majority still turn to a minister, priest or rabbi when they decide to wed. More than half the number of marriages which took place in England and Wales in 1988 were solemnized according to religious rites.

But, traditional though they may be, church weddings do not have to follow one standard, conventional type. In recent years many churches, and individual ministers, have re-thought the form for marriage services, and in many denominations today there is more room than ever before for couples to change, adapt and mould the service to make it reflect their own partnership and make it more truly *theirs*.

If you're not a regular churchgoer, the thought of having to come up with ideas for a religious service might sound a bit daunting. But it is worth spending some time thinking about it, and asking your partner for his or her views. Your ideas need not, after all, concern the purely religious side of the ceremony; you might feel that including some secular material, for example poetry or prose readings, would make the wedding more meaningful. As we will discuss further later on in this chapter, many ministers of all denominations are willing to entertain ideas for non-religious readings and music within a religious ceremony.

Nor do church ceremonies have to follow tradition to the letter when it comes to the bride arriving in the church on her father's arm or being 'given away'. For some people, of course, these long-established customs are almost as important a part of the ceremony as the vows themselves, and symbolize a meaningful link with the past. But for an increasing number of people, the notions of 'ownership' of women from which these traditions spring have become

29

recognizably outdated. Ministers, as well as couples, have come to realize that some brides no longer want to be 'handed over' by their father to their husband; quite apart from the sexist overtones of the practice, brides may wish to acknowledge the not insignificant role their mothers, as well as their fathers, played in their upbringing.

One couple I spoke to, Sophie and Paul, had been very concerned at their wedding to include only traditions which seemed really relevant to their lives. Here is how they adapted their service, which was at a Catholic church:

We looked very carefully at the traditions which are usually associated with getting married in a church. We didn't want to get rid of any parts of the ceremony just for the sake of it, but nor did we want any part of our wedding to have no significance to us. We based our service on a Mass, but we had two readings from the Indian poet Tagore. He has always been special for us: I'm half Indian, and Paul and I spent a year working together in India some time ago. We also had a poem from T. S. Eliot, because it had been a great favourite of mine for many years.

I didn't want to be given away, because we wanted to stress our equality in the relationship from the start. So Paul and I arrived at the church together, about half an hour before anyone else, and stood at the door as people came in and welcomed them. When everyone was there, we walked up the aisle together, followed by both sets of parents.

We faced everyone to say our vows, with the priest standing next to us, which I thought was enormously important. It's such a good idea to do it that way – if you stand with your backs to people, you feel isolated and apart from your family and friends. Afterwards so many people came up to us and said they felt really involved during our ceremony, and I'm sure that was why.

Sophie, 25, a potter; married Paul, 25,
a hostel worker, in May 1990

Sophie and Paul also tried to give all four parents a role in their wedding, by including the following words in their service immediately before taking their vows:

Sophie and Paul: We would like to ask our parents to join us for the cermony of marriage. It is they who have enabled us to reach this point of commitment in our lives, by their own commitment to each other and to us.
(*Parents join Sophie and Paul at front of church*).
Sophie and Paul: We ask our parents to entrust to us the loving care and responsibility that they have shown for us.
Paul's parents: We entrust to Sophie the responsibility of caring for Paul, our son, and we welcome her into our family.
Sophie's parents: We entrust to Paul the responsibility of caring for Sophie, our daughter, and we welcome him into our family.

This couple, Sophie and Paul, would clearly not have felt able to take part in a church service which included traditions which they considered outdated. But many other couples, though aware of the old-fashioned nature of much that is involved in a church wedding, decide nevertheless to opt for it. Here is how one woman described her decision to go along with the customs in their entirety:

I'm generally fairly feminist in my outlook, and often take exception to sexist symbols, but I have to admit that I knowingly went through the whole traditional wedding service without changing very much at all. Part of the reason, I suppose, was that I wasn't really aware of the possibilities of adapting it, and the priest who married us certainly didn't suggest any adaptations, even though I should think he would have agreed to anything we'd suggested. At the same time, though, I have to admit that part of me wanted the big white wedding, despite it being outdated and sexist in many ways. After my wedding, a friend who'd got married in a fairly plain ceremony without

31

a white dress or any of the trimmings told me she wished she'd done it all 'properly' at her wedding. And I suppose that's it, really: you only get one chance to have the big traditional do, and if you decide on something different you risk regretting it later on. Also, I knew our parents would be happy if we had a traditional wedding, and that was quite an important factor, too.

Anna

Music and readings

As we have already noted, there is no need to have wholly religious music or readings in many religious weddings. However, if your wedding is to be held in a place of worship, you will probably want to include at least some hymns and traditional music and a Bible reading or two.

Organists are, of course, the musicians most usually present at weddings, but they are not the only possibility. Many ministers will allow violinists, trumpeters, even small bands into the church for wedding services, although it is important to ensure that the accompanying instruments are suitable for the kind of songs or hymns you choose. If at all possible, it's often a good idea to have a choir. If the church where your wedding is being held doesn't have a choir of its own, ask the vicar or priest if he knows of a nearby church with a choir you could ask along.

There are several opportunities during most church wedding services for music. The first is at the bride's entrance (the processional), when *The Bridal March* ('Here comes the Bride') from *Lohengrin* by Wagner is popular, if a little hackneyed. Alternatives include Handel (*Water Music* – Hornpipe in D, Hornpipe in F, Coro or Minuet No. 2); Purcell (Rondeau from *Abdelazar*); Brahms (Theme from the 'St Anthony' Chorale); Parry (*Bridal March*); Mendelssohn (Organ Sonata No. 3) or Charpentier (Prelude to his *Te Deum*).

The second major chance for a piece of classical music occurs when the bride and bridegroom sign the register. As this usually happens out of sight (often in the vestry or sacristy), it is likely to capture more of the congregation's attention than the other music during the service, so it is worth putting a bit of effort into finding a good piece. There are, of course, any number of possibilities: the long list includes J. S. Bach's 'Sheep may safely graze'; Schumann's 'Träumerei'; Brahms' 'Behold, a rose is blooming', and MacDowell's 'To a wild rose'.

The list of suitable hymns for weddings is endless. You might like to get ideas from other couples' orders of service (ask the vicar if he has some, if you don't have any from friends' weddings). Among the all-time favourites are 'Lead us, Heavenly Father, lead us', 'Praise my soul the King of Heaven', and 'Love Divine all loves excelling'. As a general rule, it's a good idea to have at least one very well-known hymn to encourage members of the congregation to join in.

The final piece of music, the recessional, is played as the bride and bridegroom leave the church after the ceremony, and should reflect some of the jubilation of that moment. The most common choice is the Wedding March from *A Midsummer Night's Dream* by Mendelssohn, although Widor's *Toccata* from Symphony No. 5 is also popular and other possibilities include Fletcher's *Festive Toccata* and Whitlock's *Fanfare*.

As with music, there are several well-used Bible passages which often get an airing at weddings. These include 1 Corinthians 13 ('And the greatest of these is love . . .'); John 15. 8–12 ('Love one another as I have loved you . . .'); John 2. 1–12 (Wedding feast at Cana) and Matthew 5. 1–12 (the Beatitudes). However, you might like to spend a bit of time selecting a less obvious Bible reading: the Old Testament Song of Songs, for example, though quite seldom used at wedding services, is a collection of love poems and hence extremely suitable.

An Anglican church wedding

Most people who get married according to a religious rite in

Britain do so in an Anglican church. As it's the established religion of the land, the Church of England gets lots of not-very-devout types turning up on its doorstep asking for weddings, as well as very committed Anglicans.

However, although it is the established church, Anglican vicars are not obliged to marry anyone and everyone. To qualify for marriage in one of its churches, you should:

(a) live within its parish boundaries;
(b) be a regular worshipper there, in which case you are eligible to go on its electoral roll; or
(c) be willing to live in the parish during the three weeks when your banns are called.

In addition, either you or your partner or both of you should be baptized Christians. If neither of you has been baptized, marriage in a church is not out of the question, but it could present difficulties.

If you want to get married in a church where neither you nor your partner nor either of your families is known, it could be rather difficult to arrange. Many Church of England vicars, particularly those whose churches are pretty and photogenic, believe they get more than their fair share of weddings and are not overkeen on doing ones they are not bound to do. So if there's no reason for you to want to get married in a church other than that you think it looks an attractive place, you might be in for short shrift from the minister.

A much more likely scenario will be that you wish to get married in a church where one of your families – most often, the bride's – live, but in which neither of you are actually resident yourselves. If this is your situation, the best thing to do is to arrange to see the vicar and explain your position honestly to him (or her – you may find yourself in a parish which is run by a woman deacon, who is also able to conduct weddings). Most ministers will be sympathetic, although they will quite probably ask you to attend services at the church on a few occasions before the wedding, and you might also have to agree to live in the parish while the banns are called.

Banns are not the only way of obtaining the go-ahead for marriage in an Anglican church (see pages 24–5 for details of other methods), but only archbishop's licences, which are only rarely issued, would provide a way round the residence qualification. You could think about getting one of these if it is the only way to marry in the place of your choice, but the priest involved must be agreeable.

If you or your partner is divorced, you have no automatic right to be married in the Church of England, although if you can find a vicar willing to marry you (and some are), the wedding can go ahead quite legally; you should, of course, be resident in the parish or a regular worshipper there as described above. But even vicars who take a liberal line on remarriage are likely to want to question you both on your relationship to ensure that it was not the cause of the breakdown of the previous marriage or marriages – if it was, a church wedding could prove to be extremely difficult and you might have to settle for a civil ceremony, perhaps followed by a 'service of blessing', properly called a Service of Prayer and Dedication. This service, which usually includes prayers, a blessing and a gospel reading, can either be arranged so that it follows on directly from the register office, or for a different date entirely.

Despite the increasing numbers of couples who live together before marriage – some surveys have predicted that by the year 2000 a couple who do not live together before they marry will be a rarity – many vicars (though fewer and fewer) still take a dim view of the practice. If you and your partner live together, it might be worth trying to find out the views of the minister before you approach him – usually, these will be quite well-known among parishioners. But whatever he thinks, it's almost always best to be honest with him when you go along to see him. Apart from it being quite hard to hide your domestic arrangements (you will need to give the vicar your addresses, for example), it could lead to embarrassment during the actual wedding ceremony.

Pre-marriage preparation takes several different forms in the Church of England. If you're getting married in a larger parish with a busy vicar you might find you actually book your ceremony with someone else – the verger, for example, or a secretary. You may not meet the vicar until perhaps three months or so before the actual wedding for a couple of chats about yourselves, your religious beliefs, and your thoughts on the content of the service.

In other parishes, pre-marriage preparation is taken much more seriously, and you may find you are invited to take part in a course run by laypeople and involving perhaps three or four other couples. More and more Anglican churches, particularly evangelical ones, are running pre-marriage courses. They might include several evening meetings, or perhaps a weekend and are likely to concentrate on encouraging you to think about your relationship and future together. Most people are initially a bit apprehensive about taking part in a pre-marriage course, but those who go along usually say afterwards that it was helpful, even if only in making you aware that you are not alone in your doubts, fears, hopes and ideas for married life!

Or you may find yourself getting married in a parish where the vicar takes quite a keen interest in marriage preparation himself, and will therefore ask to see you a number of times in the weeks and months leading up to the ceremony. These occasions may turn out to be primarily times when the vicar will want to talk to you about your religious beliefs, or you may find the minister is more interested in hearing about your hopes for your marriage.

The Anglican service

Whatever the system of marriage preparation in the parish where you are to be wed, you should certainly make sure you spend some time talking to the vicar about the service itself. Basically, there are two service possibilities in the Church of England, and which you choose is up to you. The more old-fashioned is the Prayer Book service – not, usually, the 1662 version which bluntly recommends marriage as against fornication, but the so-called Series 1 service, which dates back to a

1928 revision of the Book of Common Prayer although it was not actually ratified until 1966. This service allows the bride the choice of whether or not to promise to obey her husband.

The second, and increasingly common, wedding service used in the Church of England is that introduced in 1978, the modern service. This allows the possibility of choosing and writing your own prayers, and is definitely the one to go for if you are interested in putting your individual stamp on the service in this way. Before making up your mind which service to opt for, try to read through both and see which one makes more sense to you and is more meaningful to your situation.

If you feel strongly that there are other things not contained in either service which you would like to say to one another during your wedding service, you should ask your vicar about the possibility of making additional statements. Many ministers will allow this, and will probably ask you to make them at the end of the service.

You should also ensure you talk to the vicar about flowers, music (see pages 32–3) photography and videos (see pages 62–3), and fees. You should also ensure you arrange to hold a rehearsal at the church the week or even the day before the wedding, and make sure all the principal people involved, including attendants and readers, are there.

The vicar's view

Unfortunately, vicars often feel taken for granted by couples who come along expecting them to fall over backwards to fit in with their wedding plans. Try to be sensitive to the feelings of the minister who is going to officiate at your marriage: a good relationship between priest and couple is one of the major factors in creating a good atmosphere in the church on the day. Here is one vicar's advice on how to go about befriending your minister:

People often get on the wrong side of the minister by assuming they can get married on a certain day at a certain time. They don't seem to realize that the church has a life of its own and that if they are seeking to get married according to its rites, they will have to fall in with that. They really shouldn't come along expecting it's their right to get married on Easter Saturday or something like that.

Another thing that gets up vicars' noses is the idea some couples seem to have that they are 'buying' their wedding from the church, and that they therefore have consumers' rights to do what they want with it. The church's view is that the standard fee merely covers the work involved – it is not a profit-making exercise for the vicar, and he is likely to resent being treated as if it were.

A Methodist church wedding

Methodist weddings are very similar to those of the Church of England, and most other Free Churches follow more or less the same form.

As with most Christian denominations, Methodist ministers may be reluctant to marry you unless at least one of you has been baptized. Usually, couples also have some connection with the Methodist church.

Methodist ministers are likely to be quite flexible about allowing couples to choose readings, including secular readings, and may allow them to use their own prayers.

Like their Anglican counterparts, Methodist ministers have the right to refuse marriage to couples where one or both partners have been married before, although in practice they have a reputation for being very understanding and sympathetic, and certainly their Church allows for the possibility of remarriage. Like the Anglicans, too, they do have a service of blessing which can be used if either the couple or the minister think it would be more appropriate in their case.

A Catholic church wedding

A generation ago, Catholics almost always married other Catholics; indeed, as recently as 1970 Pope Paul VI wrote of the importance of discouraging what he called 'mixed marriages', unions between Catholics and people of either another Christian denomination or no faith at all. Today, however, the ground has shifted and, particularly in Britain, marriages which take place in Catholic churches are increasingly of the 'mixed' variety.

Catholics are not, however, bound to marry in a Catholic church. If you would prefer to hold your ceremony in a church of your partner's denomination, you can ask permission to do so, via your parish priest, from the local bishop. Or you might want the minister from your partner's church to take part in your Catholic ceremony, which can also be arranged.

To be eligible to marry in a Catholic church, at least one member of the partnership must have been baptized into the faith. Some priests also ask for proof of commitment to the Church, but technically this is no reason to refuse you the right to marry; if a priest tries to do this you are entitled to appeal to the local bishop.

The Catholic Church does not usually marry couples where one or both partners have been divorced. It does, however, have its own procedure for annulling previous marriages where it can be proved before an ecclesiastical tribunal that the union was null from the start. The process is a complex and time-consuming one, but once an annulment has been granted the individuals concerned are free in the eyes of the Church to marry again.

In the past, parish priests were the only people usually involved in preparing young couples for marriage in the Catholic Church, but in recent times more and more clerics (particularly the more open-minded among them) have become aware of a certain amount of irony in the idea of them, as celibate, single men, giving advice on the state of matrimony. As a result, many parishes have set up engaged couples' courses run by married laypeople. If you find yourself hoping to get married in a church which operates such a course, you will probably be strongly advised to take part in it – indeed, in more and more dioceses, attendance on such courses is even being made compulsory.

You may, understandably, feel quite uneasy about the idea of having to go along on one of these courses – particularly if you are yourself a non-Catholic. If you find the idea completely abhorrent, or if it is quite impossible for you and your partner to attend a course together because, for example, you live at opposite ends of the country, tell the priest and ask him if you can have a few sessions with him instead. But if you can summon up the courage to go along on to the preparation course, which will probably involve three or four evenings at the church hall, you may find yourself being pleasantly surprised. Most people who take part in them dread the prospect, yet the majority say afterwards that they enjoyed the experience more than they thought they would, and that it was useful and fun to meet other people in a similar position to themselves and compare notes. The courses also provide, at a time when all thoughts are focused on the wedding day itself, a chance to spend some time thinking about yourselves, your relationship, and your hopes and fears.

Expect the course to involve some quizzes and exercises, usually done quietly with your partner, as well as general chats and group discussions. Although the role of religion and Christianity in a marriage will probably be mentioned from time to time, the course is likely to concentrate more on your relationship than on your spiritual beliefs.

As well as possibly taking part in an engaged couples' course, you will certainly have at least two interviews with the priest. He will want to assure himself that you are aware of the precepts of Catholic marriage, which basically involve being serious about remaining with one another until death, being faithful to one another and being open to the idea of having children – if not straightaway, at least at some time in the future. The Catholic Church does not sanction the use of artificial contraception, although this rule is ignored by probably 80 per cent of its followers. Many priests see the contraceptive ban as an ideal which is very difficult to adhere to in practice.

The church also requires its followers to do all they can to bring up their offspring as Catholics, although a recent document on marriage published by the Bishops of England and Wales did make the point that this should only be sought for 'within the unity of the marriage' – in other words, you're not expected to jeopardize your relationship in order to ensure your children get to Mass on Sundays. However, the priest who marries you is likely to want to discuss the matter of children and their religious upbringing with you both, and is formally required to exact a promise from the Catholic partner that he or she intends to have any children baptized into the faith.

The Catholic service

The Catholic Church, unlike the Church of England, has only one rite of marriage (and, perhaps surprisingly in such an otherwise male-dominated establishment, it contains no mention of brides having to obey their husbands). But you do have a choice over which kind of service you contain the marriage within. Basically, the possibilities are a Nuptial Mass, which involves an hour-long Communion service with the exchange of vows sandwiched in the middle, or just the marriage service on its own, which is an altogether simpler, and certainly shorter, event. To qualify for a Nuptial Mass, however, the non-Catholic partner should be a baptized Christian. And whether he or she is or not, some priests advise mixed-religion couples to have a marriage service without Mass anyway, arguing that if lots of the guests are not churchgoers they are unlikely to want to sit through a long and complicated service.

The synagogue wedding

In fact, Jewish weddings – unlike those of almost every other denomination – are not restricted to a place of worship. They can take place anywhere: by a swimming pool, US-style; under a tree; or in someone's front room. And they can take place later in the evenings than other types of wedding too: the general rule is that ceremonies must be held between 8.00

am and 6.00 pm, but exceptions are made for Jewish (and also Quaker) weddings.

Despite the wide range of possibilities these special rules afford, most Jewish weddings do take place in synagogues, usually during the afternoon, and most often on a Sunday, although Tuesdays and Thursdays are weekday alternatives. Traditionally they are large – 600 guests is not unknown, though around 300 would be more common – and are occasions of great festivity. The Jewish faith, with its particular emphasis on the importance of the family unit, sees marriage – the creation of a new family unit – as an institution of the utmost importance.

Couples which include a Jew and a non-Jew will quite probably encounter difficulties if they want to get married in a synagogue. In the United States, some rabbis look favourably on such unions, but in this country 'out' marriage, as it is called, is still frowned upon. And conversion to Judaism for the non-Jewish partner is not often a possible option either, as becoming a Jew is a complicated procedure which is not particularly encouraged by the faith.

Marriage preparation for Jewish couples usually takes the form of one or two meetings with the rabbi concerned, who will often be a family friend. About 20 per cent of couples also opt to join an engaged couples' course, which will probably be run by other couples rather than by a religious leader.

We went on an engaged couples' course run by the Jewish Marriage Council. There were about seven couples in the group, and they were of different shades of religious opinion. We talked about all sorts of things – how to manage money after we were married, whether to keep a kosher home or not. The course was held over two days and we didn't know anyone else there before we started, but we found we made friends quickly and were able to share our plans and ideas with them. It was really useful to know that there were others out there who were going through the same sorts of things we were, and it was also quite reassuring because we found we had already discussed most of the issues which came up at the preparation course, so we felt we were probably on the right lines.

Nicholas, 27, an antiques restorer; married
for two years to Fiona, 24, who works in publishing.
The couple live in North London

Talking Points

● Do you think going to church and/or praying at home are important? If so, explain to your partner why you think worship matters, and ask for his or her views. You don't have to feel exactly the same way about these issues, but it is vital for each of you to know the other's views and be prepared to respect them.

● Do you intend to pass on your religious beliefs to your children? If so, will this involve having them baptized? And how and from whom do you hope your children will learn about God, and about what is right and what is wrong in life?

● If yours is to be a religious wedding you will be asking God to bless your marriage. Do you expect God to have a place in your relationship thereafter? Will you ask God to help you in your marriage in the months and years ahead? Do you believe there are ways in which God will be present in your marriage relationship, and ways in which he will use you as a couple to further his work?

Useful Addresses

The Catholic Marriage Advisory Council, Clitherow House, 1 Blythe Mews, Blythe Road, London W14 0NW

Jewish Marriage Council, 23 Ravenshurst Avenue, London NW4 4EL

4

The Civil Service

The register office wedding

If and when the changes to the marriage laws proposed in the 1990 White Paper come into being, one of the reforms will be to extend the options of where civil marriage ceremonies may take place. Each district is then likely to provide, as well as the register office wedding room, one or two other possibilities – a local stately home, perhaps, or an impressive municipal building. Research has shown that there is much support for this move among couples, many of whom feel unhappy about the lack of choice involved in a non-religious wedding. More choice will mean more cost, of course, a fact that has led some registrars to worry that the reforms may create a 'two-tier' system in which those who can afford it will be married 'with all the trimmings' in a fairytale location, while those with fewer funds will have to make do with a register office which is not likely to have seen a lick of paint for many moons. Even at the moment, a depressing number of them tend to be rather dingy and sad-looking.

Not that register offices are always unpleasant places, of course. Many, in fact, are quite plush, attractive buildings. If you want to, ask the staff when you go to give notice if you can see the wedding room where your ceremony will take place. And if you think it could do with a bit of decoration, you could always ask whether you could provide a flower arrangement or two to brighten it up. Surprisingly few couples think of decorating the register office in this way, although of course the tradition of decking out churches with flowers for weddings remains as strong as ever. But at least two registrars I spoke to said they would have no objection to flowers being put in the wedding room by a couple.

Having a church wedding involves at least two or three meetings with the minister and often many more, but if you get married in a register office the chances are that you won't meet the person who will conduct your ceremony until a few minutes before it begins. Some people don't seem to mind this at all, but if it makes you worried, nervous or unhappy, do ask to be introduced to the registrar well in advance of the day itself. You may have to be quite determined if you want to do this; as far as registrars are concerned, weddings are everyday events, and you and your partner are just one of tens, even hundreds, of couples they'll be dealing with in a particular week. But while they might be nonchalant about your wedding, you have every right to want it to go exactly the way you want, and that may mean talking things through well before you turn up on the doorstep in your best suit and white dress.

It's certainly worth having some idea of what's likely to happen at the ceremony itself. Usually, the form is for the couple to arrive in the wedding room first, followed by their family and friends. There's no reason to stick to this pattern, though; if you want, you can assemble the guests, bridegroom and best man first and have the bride arrive in on her father's arm in traditional style. Or the couple may prefer to walk into the room together, after the guests. Generally, though, the superintendent registrar (that's the person who actually performs the marriage) comes in last of all, although the registrar is already in the room with the papers ready to be signed.

The ceremony will begin with a few words of introduction from the superintendent registrar. This will probably be brief, and will include a reminder that the office is sanctioned for marriages, and that the present assembly is gathered to celebrate the wedding of John Smith and Jenny Brown or whoever. Next, the bride and groom declare that there is no lawful impediment to the marriage and call upon the people present to witness their undertaking. The superintendent registrar will then ask them to join hands while each speaks the words which constitute the marriage contract itself, saying in turn: 'I call upon these persons here present to witness that I, John Smith, do take thee, Jenny Brown, to be my lawful wedded wife', and vice versa. The wedding ring or rings are usually exchanged at this point, and the register is then signed.

The usual procedure at a civil ceremony is for the man to make his vows first, followed by the woman, but if you're concerned about sexist overtones you might want to change this so that the bride makes hers first. Another thing to be wary of on the sexism front is the superintendent registrar who announces gustily at every wedding he performs that 'Miss Brown will now sign the register using her maiden name for the last time. . . .' If you're not planning to change your name, it's probably worth mentioning it to the registrar before the ceremony.

The entire ceremony is unlikely to last longer than ten minutes – in some busy offices on Saturdays, quarter-hour 'slots' are all the time allowed per wedding. But many small, rural offices are more flexible about time. Again, it's worth finding out whether there will be any kind of 'limit' in force on the day your ceremony is planned for. And even if there isn't, you should beware of arriving late. Punctuality may not be the first requirement of the folklore bride, but the registrar of the '90s will not be one bit impressed to be kept waiting.

If you think music would be appropriate at your ceremony, you can ask the registrar for permission to bring a cassette recorder along and have music at the beginning or end of the ceremony. But you aren't allowed to have any hymns or any kind of religious music at all, as civil marriages must, by law, be entirely secular. This regulation will continue to apply even after the new Marriage Act comes into force, although the new legislation may allow for poems or short prose readings to be made.

Register offices don't normally allow photographs to be taken during the actual ceremony, or during the signing of the register, although they will let you do a mock-up for pictures afterwards. However, this too may change, as may the old ban on video recordings at civil weddings. Until now, these have been disallowed on the grounds that as a marriage is contracted when the vows are spoken, a video which revealed that one partner stumbled over his or her words could, in theory, constitute grounds for declaring the wedding null and void!

Of crucial importance at the register office wedding, and sadly an element sometimes overlooked, is the number of guests which can be accommodated during the ceremony itself. Fire regulations often mean officials are posted at doorways to count the number of guests arriving, and they are under strict instructions to allow not one more than the room can safely hold. This can have disastrous consequences if it results in Aunt Agnes from Australia being barred from the ceremony after she's spent her life savings getting over from Sydney to see her beloved godson tie the knot, so beware. Make sure you're clear from the outset how many guests you will be able to invite, and don't be tempted to go over the limit. You should also check whether all the guests will be able to sit down or not, as if seats are limited you will have to ensure that the right people get the chairs.

Guests often get really unhappy if there's not enough room for them all to sit down. Most offices have space for some chairs, but many of those present are likely to find themselves on their feet throughout the ceremony. The couple will have been told this before the event, but often they ignore it and just invite lots of people along all the same, thinking they won't mind standing at the back. Well, take it from me that unfortunately they often do mind, and their dissatisfaction can spoil the whole do for everyone. You're often in a fairly small, confined room for the wedding, and the mood of the guests is an extremely important factor in how the whole thing goes off. My advice would be not to pack people in. Go for a few less people and try to create an intimate atmosphere. If you manage to get it right, I'm convinced a register office wedding can be a beautiful occasion. I've done lots of ones which have been significant and meaningful – I've some-times even had a lump in my throat myself.

Superintendent Registrar in a rural office

The humanist wedding

White weddings, as more and more couples are discovering, don't have to involve God. In the old days, if you wanted a big do with a posh frock and all the trimmings, chances are that a church (with God inevitably thrown in) would become the only option. But these days humanist weddings, which give scope for a meaningful, spiritual service without the hypocrisy, as many see it, of a church wedding, are becoming ever more popular. If you don't believe in God and/or don't go to church, but want your wedding to be a significant occasion which reflects your interests and your partnership, a humanist ceremony could be for you.

> I had imagined getting married in church, but somehow I just knew it wouldn't be right. I never went near a church normally, so why go to one for my wedding? But the only other option, a register office, seemed really dull. I spent ages thinking about what else we could do, and then one day I came across an article on humanist ceremonies. After I'd finished reading it, I was so happy I cried. I just knew it was what I'd been trying to find for so long.
>
> *Anne, 28, a TV researcher. Married Jonathan, 35,*
> *a film-maker, in a humanist ceremony six months ago.*

A humanist wedding means, quite simply, a marriage which does not include any mention of God or religion. It offers endless scope for creativity, because essentially it is up to you to invent the kind of wedding you want. Unlike those who choose to marry according to the rites of a particular denomination or creed, in a humanist service you are completely free to do your own thing.

It is very important to realize from the outset, however, that your humanist wedding will not have any meaning in a legal sense, so you will need to have a separate civil ceremony in a register office. (Unless, of course, you decide that you do not want to be married at all in a legal sense, but that you just want to gather your relatives and friends and make them aware of your commitment to one another.)

You should not be put off by the fact that the humanist ceremony does not comprise a legal contract. Although it might sound difficult in practice to make everyone aware of the importance and significance of a non-legal service, many couples have managed to do it very successfully. In many continental countries, after all, marriage still consists of two different ceremonies, one legal and one religious, and the duality of the occasion does not in any way undermine it. Many couples choose not to exchange rings at the register office, saving that part for their 'real' ceremony.

We went along to the register office on the morning of our wedding day, and had our humanist ceremony in the early evening. We were very keen that everyone should see the evening as the important bit, so although we're both very close to our families, we only took our two best friends along to the register office and we didn't dress up – Jonathan didn't even bother to wear a tie. In a way, I suppose, we looked on the register office ceremony as a private part of our wedding and the evening ceremony as the public part.

Anne

Where you decide to hold your humanist ceremony is, of course, up to you. Anne and Jonathan were keen to find somewhere beautiful with a sense of history. After a long search, they decided to hire a local museum. Other couples I met had been married in humanist ceremonies held in hotels, stately homes and even Unitarian churches – some Unitarian ministers are willing to act as celebrants, and will even promise not to mention God once!

Organizing a humanist ceremony can seem a bit daunting, as you're virtually being presented with a blank page. Many couples find it useful to contact the British Humanist Association, whose address is at the end of this chapter, for advice and information about what kind of format a humanist wedding can take. The association can also help provide you with a celebrant to conduct the service, although you might prefer to ask a friend or member of your family. Most couples end up with a service based on a Humanist Association outline, but with many of their own touches. It can be as traditional, as inventive, or as outrageous as you choose.

Our ceremony was a very traditional affair; although there wasn't one mention of God, in all other ways it was very like a church wedding. I wore a long, white dress and Jonathan was in a morning suit. We were both very clear about what we wanted the ceremony to include, and the celebrant, who was a member of the BHA, was very accommodating and never once said we couldn't do this or we couldn't do that. We felt he was really with us and as keen as we were for the wedding to reflect us and who we were.

In deciding what we actually wanted to say to one another in our vows, we looked at the conventional church vows and worked our way through them, deciding what we wanted to jettison and what we wanted to keep in. We didn't want any mention of God – we felt it was up to us to make the marriage work rather than the idea that God was going to shower blessings down on us. We both believe that our responsibility in life is to one another, not to God. And we were able to reflect all that in our vows.

Anne

Deciding what you want to promise to one another in your vows is a very personal choice, but you might find it useful to know the sorts of vows other couples have chosen to make to one another. Sarah, a 28-year-old secretary, and Martin, a 35-year-old systems analyst, wrote the following words for their service:

Celebrant (a member of the BHA): Martin, do you take Sarah to be your wife, to share your life with her, and do you pledge that you will love, respect and tenderly care for her in all the varying circumstances of your lives?
Martin: Yes, I do.

Celebrant: Sarah, do you take Martin to be your husband, to share your life with him, and do you pledge that you will love, respect and tenderly care for him in all the varying circumstances of your lives?

Sarah: Yes, I do.

Celebrant: Here today Martin and Sarah proclaim their love to the world, and we who are gathered here rejoice with them and for them in the new life they now undertake together.

Another couple, who were married amid the splendour of a castle, exchanged the following vow, stressing their need for independence:

I freely make this choice to be with you. I acknowledge the difficulties and truly believe this to be a solemn undertaking. I value our independence and I will work towards our growth both as individuals and as a couple, to enhance the intimacy we share. I give to you without question honest fidelity, and an openness to share and to support throughout our lives together. As a sign of my love I place this ring on your finger.

A humanist wedding also means you have plenty of scope for music and prose and poetry readings. Martin and Sarah chose the following lines, taken originally from an American Indian ceremony:

Now you will feel no rain
for each of you will be shelter for the other.
Now you will feel no cold
for each of you will be warmth to the other.
Now there is no more loneliness.
Now you are two persons,
but there is only one life before you.
Go now to your dwelling
to enter into the days of your life together.

Again, the choice of whether to have a reading and what to have is in your hands. Many couples like to choose pieces which reflect their own interests and experiences, and perhaps their hopes for their life together.

Attendants

Whatever the type of ceremony, most brides and bridegrooms recruit a few friends to help them cope with the preparations and to ensure things go smoothly on the great day. There are no special rules about who these people should be. Traditionally, they have tended to be unmarried friends, but these days it often seems rather odd for a best friend not to be eligible to be best man merely because he himself got married a few months ago instead of just living with his girlfriend. Rather than looking at your potential helpers' marital status, be guided by how well you know them, and whether you really trust them.

Etiquette books have fairly definite roles to assign to particular attendants, but there is no need to be dictated to by rigid rules on the matter of who does what. However, what is important is that everyone who has something to do is clear about what their task is. Otherwise, you will find people tripping over one another to show Great Aunt Madge to her seat in the church, but no one to drive her to the reception.

Choose your attendants carefully, and be clear about what you expect of them, and you will be amazed at how wonderful friends can be.

The best man is, perhaps, the most celebrated attendant at a wedding. Traditionally, he was required to arrange the stag night, drive the groom to the wedding, and to pass the wedding ring to the celebrant during the ceremony. Other roles earmarked for him include paying the vicar's fees (the bridegroom was supposed to pay him back later), supervising the ushers, and arranging the transport to the reception. However, the most important part of being a best man has always been, and is still, his duty to support his friend the bridegroom in the busy build-up to the wedding day, and on the day itself.

Best men almost always say at least a few, and often a great many, words at the wedding reception, traditionally chronicling in witty style the bridal couple's romance and path to the altar. The thought of having to make a speech is often one of the most stomach-churning elements of the entire day for the best man, bridegroom, bride's father, bride, and anyone else who is to make one but, say most of those whose ordeal has gone before, the experience is often not half as terrifying as you might anticipate. Here's one best man's advice:

> All best men are nervous about making their speech, but the important thing to remember is that the guests – the audience – are on your side. They want to laugh at your jokes and enjoy your tales, and you don't have to be an amazingly brilliant speaker to get a good reception. Just keep it fairly simple, try not to be too long-winded, and throw in a few jokes – that's all it takes.

The best man's speech usually comes after those of the bride's father (who traditionally kicks the proceedings off by proposing a toast to the couple) and that of the bridegroom, who usually thanks the host(s) for the reception, thanks the guests for the presents, and toasts the bridesmaids. Traditionally, he speaks on behalf of himself and his new wife, but these days many wives decide to say a few words themselves, unwilling to allow themselves to be seen as their husband's silent shadow.

The best man's speech tends to follow that of the bridegroom and bride, if she is making one. Again, there is a sexist element to his speech as he is supposedly replying to the bridegroom's toast on behalf of the bridesmaids. However, this is increasingly seen as rather anachronistic, and many best men make no reference to the bridesmaids, who may, in any case, want to speak themselves.

Bridesmaids continue to feature at most weddings, and are

often teenage relatives of the bride or bridegroom. They are expected to help the bride get herself ready for the church, but in reality have little function save to look pretty on the photographs. Some brides have decided, in fact, that the job of bridesmaid can be perfectly well performed by an animal: poodle Jemma, dyed a delicate shade of pink for the day, trotted up the aisle behind her owner, Kathy Starling of Scarborough, at her wedding in June 1990. Because it's so much about appearances, many couples ask quite young children – boys as well as girls – to follow them up the aisle. But be warned, very young children, especially those under four, are really too small to be expected to cope with doing as they're told and sitting still through a service, and bawling toddlers with red eyes won't be much of an asset when it comes to the pictures.

Popular though bridesmaids will almost certainly continue to be, their role is to some extent being usurped by the addition of a best woman at a small but growing number of weddings. Best women are seen as an altogether more grown-up and equal supporter for the bride. Because they're not an established part of the wedding set-up, the role of best woman is one unfettered by the demands of etiquette, so it's up to you and your best woman to devise what she does and when. Here's what one woman who performed the role thought of it:

Being a best woman certainly didn't mean just standing around looking pretty. I saw my job as making sure things ran smoothly, so I checked the bridesmaids were OK and tried to make sure everything was going to plan. What I didn't want to do was walk up the aisle in a silly dress, which seems a bit daft when you're nearly 30. But I stood beside the couple when they said their vows, and I handed the bridegroom's ring to the minister during the service. I also made a speech at the reception, which I think is very important indeed – women should be seen making speeches on these occasions. Overall, I think being a best woman meant playing a more positive role in the whole event, being someone who was making things happen rather than just the passive onlookers which bridesmaids can so often be.

The faraway wedding

Have you ever dreamed of getting married on a beautiful sunny beach on a far-off island? The idea has its attractions for most of us, particularly during those hectic months when there seem to be a million things to do if your wedding day is ever going to happen. But some people are really serious about the idea of away-from-it-all nuptials with the minimum of fuss, the maximum of good weather, and not much more cost involved than that of the average long-haul honeymoon. And what's more, their dream can now come true, thanks to the growth, over the last decade or so, of holiday companies which can make all the arrangements for a wedding abroad.

The idea appeals to all sorts of couples for different reasons, but seems to be particularly suitable in cases where one or both partners have been married before and may feel they have already 'done' the white wedding with all the trimmings, so want something more quiet and private this time around. Cost might also influence the choice of a faraway wedding. And sometimes couples whose families have 'difficult' circumstances – recent rows which threaten to overshadow any large gathering of the clans, for example – may decide to opt for marriage overseas.

The process is, in fact, surprisingly easy. You will need to get hold of the brochure of one of the companies which specializes in weddings abroad, and will then be able to choose your destination just as you would choose any ordinary holiday. The Caribbean is the most popular venue for British couples marrying abroad, but Bali or Miami are other possibilities. Some companies will entertain any idea you have to get married anywhere in the world, and will produce a tailor-made package for you if your idea is at all feasible, although this option will of course be more expensive than something more run-of-the-mill.

Companies which arrange weddings overseas undertake to do all the legal work involved on your behalf, and will ask you to send photocopies of relevant documents to them after you have made your booking. However, you will still have to take the originals of these documents with you to show to the local registrar before your wedding. Do make sure you have all the necessary pieces of paper before you set off, and doublecheck with the company exactly what you'll need to have with you.

Each country has its own regulations on how long you need to be resident before you can get married there, so you will usually have to wait a few days before your ceremony. You will probably have to have one brief meeting with a lawyer a couple of days before the ceremony, and you should also get a chance to meet the registrar or celebrant to discuss what sort of wedding you would like.

Alison, 28, a civil servant, and Bill, 24, an electrician, were married two months ago in St Lucia. They already had a home together in Manchester, and decided to get married when Alison's divorce from a previous marriage came through. A faraway wedding suited them because they did not want to put Alison's parents through the expense of a big wedding for a second time, and also because her first husband was unhappy at the idea of his and Alison's two children being involved in her marriage ceremony to Bill.

The first seven days in St Lucia were just like any ordinary holiday, really – lots of sunbathing and swimming. The wedding was on the eighth day of our stay in order to fulfil the island's residence qualification. Our ceremony was held in the hotel's garden which overlooked the sea. It was a lovely spot, and they had put lots of garlands of flowers up for us. Another couple staying at the hotel who were also from Britain and also getting married were our witnesses, although we could have had local people if we'd wanted. It was quite a simple, straightforward service lasting about 25 minutes. The registrar asked us whether we'd like a few prayers – St Lucia is a Catholic country, so they're not really used to non-religious weddings there – and we said yes, we would like some. Afterwards we had lots of photographs taken to show to our family and friends back at home – the whole thing was videotaped, too. I wore a pink suit which I'd brought along, although if I'd wanted a white dress I could have hired one from the holiday company. Afterwards we had a meal with the other couple we'd met, and then just carried on with our holiday. Getting married abroad certainly wouldn't suit everyone – if you're the kind of person who wants to be the centre of attention and have all the neighbours see you setting off to the church in a big Rolls, it's not for you. But we wanted something unfussy, relaxed and personal, and going to St Lucia certainly fulfilled our expectations.

Alison

Talking Points

● Discuss with your partner what you hope to get from your wedding ceremony, both individually and as a couple. Is the day itself going to be merely the formalizing of a way of life you have already worked out for yourselves, or do you hope it will signal the start of a new chapter in your relationship?

● What impression of yourselves and your relationship would you hope your friends and family will take away with them as they leave your wedding? What statement, if any, would you most like to make about the way of life you have chosen to lead, and the values you hold dear? The answers to these questions should help you see more clearly what kind of reception you really want.

Useful Addresses
British Humanist Association, 13 Prince of Wales Terrace, London W8 5PG

5

Memories to Treasure

Of all the professionals on whose services your wedding day will draw, two stand out as being of supreme importance: the vicar or registrar, and the photographer. Indeed, as a fellow guest at one wedding I went to not long ago pointed out as we stood around for what seemed like several hours while the photographer did his stuff outside the church, the man (or woman) behind the camera has in some ways taken over the role of prime celebrant at the late-twentieth-century marriage service. More and more often, it is the photographer whose needs seem to be paramount on the day; more and more often, the demands of the celluloid image are being allowed to dictate how and when things are done. It is almost as though the day was devoted to the production of a set of perfect pictures, rather than to the proclamation of a set of vows and the signing of a marriage certificate.

In defence of his or her work, the photographer will, of course, argue that a wedding day is only 24 hours long, and that once it is over the pictures are likely to assume a central role in prompting memories of the event. Surely, he or she will say, it is worth putting some effort (and cash) into creating a lasting record of so significant an occasion: a record you will (hopefully) want to treasure for many years to come, and no doubt to pass on one day to children and even grandchildren.

The good photographer will argue, too, that it is only a bad practitioner who will need to encroach too much on your day to produce a set of first-rate pictures. Trained, experienced wedding photographers should be able to achieve stunning pictures with the minimum of time and fuss, which is one of the reasons why, if you care about having good photographs, it is worth spending a bit of time, and perhaps a bit of extra money, on someone who is really capable of doing the job.

So how should you go about finding someone to entrust

with the job of consigning your memories to celluloid? First and foremost, if you can possibly afford it, pay for a professional: snap-happy friends and relatives are likely to come up trumps with all sorts of fun pictures which you can use for a second album afterwards, but few people would be without their paid-for pictures. Professionals know how to cope with bad weather (they will usually take the group shots and portraits in the church, often with the altar as a backdrop, if it's raining), and how to make sure all the details of that dress you paid hundreds for show up properly. Even if you discover to your horror that you've woken up covered in spots on your wedding morning, a good photographer will be able to minimize the damage for posterity.

If you or your partner have had professional photographs taken in the recent past and were pleased with the result, it could be that the photographer on that occasion would be able to cover your wedding too. If you don't know a photographer personally, try to get a recommendation from friends, particularly from friends who have used the person for their own wedding. You could also contact the Institute of Professional Photography or the Society of Wedding Photographers (addresses at the end of this chapter) for help in finding someone; both organizations provide lists of vetted photographers who specialize in weddings, and recommend people in three categories – licenceship (the primary level), associateship (the intermediate level) and fellowship (the top level).

But even a string of letters after someone's name doesn't necessarily mean he or she is the person who is right for you. To find that out, you will need to visit the photographer's studio and have a look at his or her portfolio. Look out not only for the kind of quality of pictures you're hoping for from your own wedding, but also the kind of style involved in producing them: do the shots seem starchy and formal, soppy and soft-focused, or fluid and carefree? Only choose a photographer if the style of his or her pictures matches the style you're looking for.

You should be quite sure what kind of pictures it is you're after. At the end of the day, I think there's all the difference in the world between liking what's in your wedding album and absolutely loving them. It always amazes me that people pay a fortune for the cake and the dress and then try to cut corners with the photography: when it's all over, the pictures are all you've got left.

Dennis Hylander, top wedding photographer

Planning the pictures

You will need to have at least one, and maybe two, meetings with your photographer before the day itself, both to try to get to know him or her a little and so that he or she is aware of the shots and groups you want for your album. Dennis Hylander, one of the country's leading wedding photographers and a fellow of both the Royal Photographic Society and the British Institute of Professional Photography, suggests that a good way to get to know your photographer and his or her way of working is to have some pictures taken a few months before the wedding. This will, of course, involve some extra cost but, says Mr Hylander, it's likely to pay off in terms of better pictures on the wedding day itself.

Whether you opt for pre-wedding pictures or not, you will certainly need to discuss prices at your initial meeting with the photographer. You may find yourself presented with a range of 'packages' and having to make a choice about how many pictures you want taken based on how much you want to pay. Alternatively, you may find your photographer charges a basic fee and leaves you with the option of how many pictures to choose, and how much extra cost to incur, after the event. Make sure you're quite clear what the cost you will pay includes: will the photographer take any pictures at the bride's home, for example, or will he start his shoot at the church or register office? Will more pictures be taken at the reception?

The photographer is bound to have his or her own ideas about possible portraits of the bridal couple, and you should be guided by these. Don't be afraid to make your own suggestions, too, though. And make sure the photographer knows what group shots you're keen to have taken; although he'll expect to do all the usual pictures of each family with the couple and so on, you might want to ask him to get a picture of yourself with a group of school or college friends, or a three-generation picture with your great-granny or whatever. The usual procedure is to ask you to fill these details in on a form, but if you've got a request for anything unusual it's best to bring it to the photographer's notice by mentioning it too.

You might also like to bring up at the initial meeting the question of how you'll view the pictures after the wedding. In the past, newly-returned honeymooners would usually be presented with a full set of proofs which they would tout round parents, grannies, nextdoor neighbours and work-mates before coming up with a definite order for the album. However, times are changing in the photographic world, and the advent of new technology now means it is possible to make first-rate copies from colour prints in a few hours. Although it is illegal to copy wedding pictures as the copyright belongs to the photographer and not the client, the fear that couples will do this and reduce their order accordingly means photographers are increasingly wary about allowing their prints out of the office, so you may find yourself having to go along to the studio to look at the photographs and making your decision on what will go in the album there and then. Another possibility is that the pictures may be made initially into transparencies and shown to you on a screen at the first viewing, and then only the ones you choose for your album will be made up into prints.

Also, and importantly, you must talk to your photographer about how long he or she will need to take pictures at crucial stages in the proceedings – especially outside the church. Wedding guests are as a breed a jovial, happy lot, but there's nothing like a long wait under a hot sun or on a chilly day to turn them into a crowd of malcontents. And it really isn't fair, after all, to keep people hanging about. If you must have an extended photo session, at least make sure it happens when the guests are happily ensconced at the reception, drinks in hand. According to Dennis Hylander, a photographer who knows his stuff should need no longer than half an hour outside the church to get all the shots he needs. And if you are planning to go to a park for some scenic shots en route to the reception (this is sometimes a good plan if the reception venue doesn't have particularly attractive grounds), you should elicit a promise that you won't be kept there either for longer than half an hour.

Videoing your wedding

More and more people are opting to take a moving as well as a static record of their wedding ceremony (and even their reception), although few have gone as far as to actually replace still photographs with a video as the 'official record'. However, the wedding video industry is as yet a fledgling one, and you may find it difficult to hire someone for whom you have a bona fide recommendation as you could with a photographer. This, and the high cost of employing a film crew for the day, leads many couples to decide to look on the video, if they have one at all, as the 'home movie' of their day, and ask a suitable amateur cameraman or woman to record events with a hired camera. The results can often be fun, but you should think seriously about whether you want a camera, even with your best friend or his cousin behind it, popping up in front of your nose all day. Some vicars who originally had no objection to video cameras during ceremonies are now changing their minds and banning them, on the grounds that their presence detracted too much from the service and encouraged people to 'act' instead of behaving naturally.

Video recorders are banned from register offices (although this could change under the new regulations). If you're getting married in church and the vicar will allow it, he may charge you a fee for the privilege, and will probably also encourage you to get a licence from the Mechanical Copyright Protection Society (MCPS, address at the end of this chapter), which costs a few pounds and means you cannot be held responsible for infringing the copyright of any of the hymns and music sung and played at the service.

Talking Points

● Share with your partner ideas of which groups of people you would like to be photographed with for your wedding album, and ask him/her who s/he would like included. This is an important practical exercise, as you need to have a clear idea about the groups you want photographed to pass on to your photographer well before the day; but it will also help make you more aware of the influences and characters who have helped shape both your lives.

● Talk about who has been important in your life and that of your partner. Don't be afraid to mention people who have already died as well as those who are alive now.

● Discuss what your wedding will mean to others taking part. How significant an occasion will it be for your parents and those of your partner? What do you think your friends, joint and individual, will make of it all? Although many couples fall into the trap of allowing parents to 'take over', make sure you don't go too far the other way and shut your parents out of a day they have every right to want to share.

Useful Addresses

British Institute of Professional Photography, Amwell End, Ware, Herts., SG12 9HN Tel: 0920 4011

Society of Wedding Photographers, Tel: 0372 726123

Mechanical Copyright Protection Society, 41 Streatham High Road, London SW16 Tel: 081–769 4400

6

A Feast of Ideas

In an age when large, dressy parties have become a thing of the past for all but the most upper of the upper classes, the wedding reception stands alone, an elaborate feast unrivalled in its extravagance. If anything, the fact that it has become the last bastion of the big do has made it more elaborate and extravagant, and often more expensive, than ever it used to be: a real once-in-a-lifetime, no-holds-barred event. This has its advantages. It means your big day will be a major occasion for all your guests, as well as for you and your partner. But it has its dangers too. Because people have become so unused to organizing large events, many have mistakenly come to believe that to do them 'right' they have got to have as much formality as possible. But the fact is that we live in an increasingly informal world, and formality today often appears stuffy, nonsensical, even absurd. So while most couples like to include touches of traditional formality here and there at their wedding reception, you shouldn't feel any compulsion to follow grandma's etiquette book by the letter. And above all, don't worry, and don't be talked into worrying, about what other people will think if you do things differently from the formal or traditional way. Apart from the fact that it doesn't matter a jot as long as you're happy with the way things go, how many people do you think actually know who the bridegroom is supposed to speak on behalf of, or when the cake-cutting should happen?

Just as over-formality doesn't guarantee a successful reception, so overspending doesn't necessarily create one either. Providing you plan your strategy and ensure there are a few basics to hand, there's no reason why a low-budget reception shouldn't provide just as enjoyable an afternoon or evening as one worth many thousands of pounds. Above all, the important thing is to organize an event which will reflect the people you and your partner are and the kind of relationship you have. Try not to become submerged beneath a crushing, meaningless 'etiquette': if something doesn't really suit you and your partner – for example, a receiving line at the reception – then leave it out. If your parents are keen to have one to ensure they get to meet your friends, promise them you'll spare some time to wander around introducing them to people.

All the same, it is vital to work out early on how much you or your family is prepared to spend on the party. You can then keep your plans on a realistic footing.

Where will it be?

The next decision to make is where to hold the reception. Many people like the idea of hosting it in their own home, because they think it will make for a personal atmosphere and more control over what sort of food and drink to provide. It also means you have lots more control over how long your reception goes on – one of the biggest drawbacks to a hotel is that you are almost always obliged to end at a predetermined hour, whereas if you're at home you can dance until you drop. This spontaneity and freedom means parties at home can be very successful, although for many people they are thought too difficult because of lack of space. Sometimes, though, even small houses have gardens big enough to take a marquee – but be warned, they are expensive. The cheapest option may be to go for a 'lean-to' which provides a kind of tented extension, sometimes leading out from a back door or, more usually, French windows. But the sky's the limit with marquees: if you want to spend a fortune, you can have a huge palace-under-canvas set up with chandeliers, a dance floor, even carpets.

If you don't have enough room for a reception at home, don't have enough money for a reception in a marquee, but are not keen, all the same, on finding a hotel for your party, you might want to consider hiring a room or rooms. The options on this will depend on what sort of area you live in and whether you want to find somewhere which will allow you the freedom to arrange your own food and drink, but you might find rooms available for hire in a church hall, a pub or a community centre.

Most people, though, eschew all these ideas in favour of the hotel, attracted by the knowledge that they will be able to leave much of the planning and preparation in the hands of professionals. In choosing a hotel, bear in mind that you do not want your guests to have to travel too far from the church or register office. (I went to one wedding where the bride-groom's parents managed to get lost on the ten-mile drive between the church and the hotel and didn't arrive until half way through the meal, well after the reception line they were supposed to have taken part in.) Lost in-laws aside, your guests will not enjoy having to battle with Saturday afternoon traffic and navigate complicated routes to far-off reception venues, so begin by looking at hotels in an area within easy reach of your ceremony.

When you've found a hotel which looks hopeful, go there with your partner – and your family, if they're involved in choosing where the party is to be held – and have a meal. Hotels often offer couples a dinner on the house to try out the menu they've chosen for their wedding meal, but as this will usually be after you've paid your deposit, there's not much you can do about it if you don't like what you're given. So try the place out before anyone realizes you're considering spending hundreds of pounds on a wedding reception, and spend some time sussing out what kind of place it is, whether the staff are friendly, and whether the atmosphere exudes a sense of confidence and well-being.

If none of these options sounds appealing, and you'd like a wedding party which is a bit out of the ordinary, there are all sorts of options for receptions on boats and barges, in castles and stately homes, on trains and buses – even at zoos and art galleries. Ask at your local tourist information centre about possible venues in your area, and plough through Yellow Pages for more ideas.

A sit-down meal or a buffet?

Wherever you decide you'd like your reception to be held, one of the first things you'll have to sort out is whether you want a sit-down meal or a buffet. A sit-down meal is usually more formal (though not inevitably). Many couples and their parents opt for it merely because they feel it's the 'right' thing to do. In fact there's no right or wrong about it – the poshest wedding receptions held in top London hotels are often champagne-and-canapés-only affairs, without any proper meal at all. The choice of what to eat and where to eat it is yours. Here is one bride's description of why she chose a sitdown meal:

> I was always quite certain that I wanted a sit-down meal. To be honest, I suppose part of it was that I quite liked the idea of a chance to sit on a top table. And I knew my parents would like that part of it, too. I also thought it would be more relaxing, in that Steven and I would be able to sit down properly and have a rest after the busy morning.

Another bride said consideration of elderly relatives who would not be happy standing while eating their meal had led her to opt for a sit-down meal. And several more said they thought sitting down to eat had made their event more of an occasion – a really special meal, rather than just any old party.

One drawback to sitting down, though, is that you will find you spend a large part of your day talking to your families and each other – in other words, the people you probably speak to most often anyway. If you think a wedding is essentially a family day, fine. But many couples who have sit-down receptions do say afterwards that they hadn't realized how little chance they would have to talk to their guests – particularly those who had long-lost cousins there who'd flown in from Australia, or a group of childhood friends they hadn't seen for years. Here's what a bride who opted for a buffet meal said afterwards of her reception:

We had our reception at home and a sit-down meal was out of the question as there just wasn't enough room. But I thought that was just fine, as I'd never wanted one anyway – I wanted to have as much chance as possible to talk to my family and friends. I hardly saw Simon at all during the reception, which was no problem at all – after all, we had a whole fortnight's honeymoon ahead with only each other for company. Another thing about having a buffet meal is it's likely to be cheaper, so you can spend more money on getting better food, as you're not paying for so many waiters and waitresses.

Another possible advantage of a buffet over a sit-down meal is that, if there are people coming along with different dietary needs (and apparently one in 14 of us has such needs), you can include lots of different sorts of dishes – some vegetarian, some vegan, some sugar-free or whatever – in your meal.

How to organize a reception at home or in a hired room

If you've opted to hold your reception at home or in a room you've hired, the first priority is to find yourself a good, reliable caterer. If possible it's best to have one recommended to you by someone else who's used the firm, but if you can't find one that way try looking through your local newspaper and Yellow Pages. It's a bit more difficult to try out a caterer than a hotel, but you should make sure you ask them lots of questions about previous receptions they've done, and perhaps even ask if there's someone whose party they've catered for who you could talk to.

When it comes to choosing the food, be prepared to be guided by the caterer, although if you've always known what menu you wanted for your wedding don't be put off. Most people, incidentally, decide on salmon for their main course – usually it's cold poached salmon for a buffet, and hot salmon with hollandaise sauce for a sit-down meal. Chicken is the second most popular food served. If you're keen on salmon or chicken but want to be different, why not ask about interesting sauces, or think up some exciting way of serving the vegetables or salad?

Caterers will expect to provide all the table linen, cutlery, napkins and china, and the use of these should be included in their price. You will have to make sure that either you or they ensure that essentials such as glasses, ice buckets, ice and – of course – corkscrews are not forgotten.

A home reception also gives you the chance to organize your own wine if you want to (see pages 73–4 for ideas on what to choose). This might take a bit more time, but it's likely to be financially worthwhile. As far as other drinks go, it is possible to set up a cash bar in your own home, but you must apply for an occasional licence from the local magistrates court.

How to plan a hotel reception

Once you've found a hotel you like which you know caters within your price range, make an appointment to see the banqueting manager so you can discuss prices (remember to check whether VAT and service are included in the costs you're quoted) and hear about the kinds of options and menus the hotel can offer. You should ask, too, about a room to store the presents, a room for the bride and groom to change in, and – particularly if you're planning an evening reception –whether your guests can get rooms at a special rate. Many hotels include a night at the hotel for the bride and groom themselves in the cost of the wedding reception, particularly if it's an evening party. Here's some more advice about how to handle this initial interview from the banqueting manager at a top London hotel:

Before you go along for your first meeting with the relevant staff member at the hotel you've chosen, you should have some idea about how many guests you're planning to invite, be clear about how much money you've got to spend, and have some thought of whether you'd prefer to have a buffet or a sit-down meal. But do be prepared to listen to the advice the manager gives, and if you start to feel that another option sounds more interesting than the one you had in mind, then say so and think about changing your plans. What you want to drink is another important question which you should have thought about. And you should also know whether you want the hotel to provide the cake, or whether you're getting that from somewhere else.

You will almost certainly want some flower arrangements on the tables and possibly elsewhere for your reception. The hotel may offer to do the flowers themselves, but this will probably prove more expensive than if you organized your own florist, or even did them yourself or got a friend to do them. The same is true of any musical entertainment you might want during the day or evening.

If you're very keen on a 'theme' wedding, with everything matching right through the day, you might want your order of service sheets to match your menus and place cards at the reception afterwards. In this case, you'll either have to get the hotel's printer to do your service sheets or tell the hotel that you'll get the menus done yourself.

Hotels differ in how much freedom they allow you to bring your own flowers, band and stationery, but a good hotel will be flexible. The only thing the hotel has an absolute right to insist on is that it supplies all the food and drink. If you want to change that, you shouldn't really be having your reception at a hotel in the first place.

Another thing you might be interested in finding out is how the food you choose will be presented. In the past, formal meals almost always involved silver service, with guests first being given their plates, and then their meat or fish and vegetables arriving separately. Since the advent of nouvelle cuisine, however, with its emphasis on presentation, 'plated' meals, with the main item already on the plate, has become much more common, and hopefully makes the meal look more attractive. It is not, however, the only way of presenting a meal – you might like your meat or fish carved at each table by a chef, for example.

The hotel will certainly want to give you some sort of deadline for when you must leave, and are likely to get most upset if you fail to meet it. Hotels usually welcome wedding parties on Saturday lunchtimes because there isn't much other trade around then, but Saturday nights provide big business and if a couple or their guests outstay their welcome and hog the ballroom or dining room while staff are trying to get it back into operation they will be extremely unpopular.

As far as the bill is concerned, the hotel is likely to expect you to pay a deposit when you confirm you'd like your reception with them, and then the balance a couple of weeks before the day itself. Afterwards, you'll probably have to pay a bit extra for additional drink consumed, although you can put an absolute ceiling on how much you're going to get through, in which case you must make this very clear to the catering manager.

Who should we invite?

This is the perennial tricky question. Who *do* you want there at the social event of your life? And will there be people you don't really want who nonetheless ought to be asked?

The short answer to the last question is almost certainly yes. However much you are planning a wedding which reflects you and your partner rather than your parents, there are two important factors you should not overlook. The first is that if someone else (your parents or his) are paying all or a large share of the bill for the reception, it is only fair that they have some say in who comes along. And the second point is that it is selfish to ignore the importance of your wedding day to the people who brought you into the world: although it is, or should be, very definitely your day you should recognize that it nonetheless represents a milestone in your parents' lives as well as in your own, and it is only natural for them to want to share that aspect of it with some friends of their generation.

All this does not mean, however, that you should suffer in silence if you feel your wedding day is being swamped by people you hardly know. If you feel your parents are being unreasonable in the number of people they want to invite, you may have to remind them that it is your wedding day, not theirs, and that, although you appreciate that they will want some of their own friends present, they surely understand that you want to be surrounded by people you feel close to and supported by (your own friends). You are not, after all, getting married to provide your parents with the chance of a social occasion.

Which family members to invite may also cause headaches. There is no hard and fast rule about which relatives are sufficiently distant to be discounted, because so much depends on how large or small your family is and how closely relationships are maintained. It would have been unthinkable, at our wedding, to leave out my mother-in-law's only cousin, whom she visited every fortnight; but ludicrous to start sending invitations to my father's 50 plus cousins, many of whom he had not seen since childhood. But it is sometimes worth going through a list of relatives (and friends too, for that matter) and asking yourself whether you would be offended if you did not receive an invitation to their wedding, or one in their close family. Honest answers should provide a helpful guide to who it would be alright to miss out.

You should also be aware, while making your list, of the social groups you are creating. (This matters too, of course, when you come to drawing up your seating plan, if you're having a sit-down reception.) Weddings, in my experience, are always best if you know a reasonable number of the other guests so try to avoid, if at all possible, inviting individuals who are completely isolated from all the other social groups there. A sizeable group of closely-knit friends – who know, if possible, both bride and groom – are a great asset at a wedding reception, particularly during the speeches when they can be relied upon to provide some heckling and banter.

Another decision you will have to make is whether or not to invite small children. To a large extent this depends very much on whether or not there are children close to you, both in your family and among your friends. If you do not have any nieces or nephews or close friends with children, and particularly if you are having a long service and/or a reception which you feel would be unsuitable for children, it is quite acceptable to decide against inviting any along: simply make your feelings known generally, and only include adults' names on your invitations.

What to drink

As Oscar Wilde once said, there's only one thing worse than a wedding with bad wine, and that's a wedding with no wine at all. Drink is very important at a reception; surprisingly, many couples who spend hours deciding on their menus give hardly any thought at all to what their guests will wash their food down with. But you shouldn't let the fact that you might not know a lot about wine put you off reading a bit about it and taking advice on which sort would go best with the food you're planning to serve.

Here are some pointers to how to solve the drink problem at your wedding party:

• If you're buying your own wine, go along to a good wine merchants or chain shop and ask the manager or one of his or her staff for advice. If your reception is at a hotel, ask the wine waiter for help.

• Keep in mind that you're catering for a wide range of ages and tastes. Sancerre or Sauvignon might be the only white wine you'd touch, but if you suspect his grandma goes for sweet German it's only kind to get a few bottles of that, too.

• Pimms, sherry or sparkling wine are the usual choices for an aperitif when your guests first arrive. Champagne is, of course, fine too, but due to the huge explosion in demand of late (Britons managed to down 23 million bottles in 1989 alone) prices are now sky high and you may quite probably decide to serve it only with the speeches at the end of the meal, if at all. The word is that smart people are turning their backs on champagne, and moving instead onto the new kinds of sparkling white wines being developed in Spain (try Raimat Chardonnay and Codorniu Chardonnay) and Australia (try Angas Brut NV and Seaview Pinot Noir/Chardonnay). These and many others of the same ilk are said to be as good as champagne despite costing only about a third of the price.

Baking your cake

Cakes have been a traditional wedding reception centrepiece since the seventeenth century, when small spiced buns would be piled up and covered with a crust of sugar. Over the years the icing of the wedding cake has become more and more of an art, and today it is possible to have a cake iced in all sorts of elaborate and intricate designs. You can also choose, of course, how many tiers to have, and will be asked whether you want the cakes arranged on columns in traditional style, or piled directly on top of one another, which can look extremely attractive. (However many tiers you decide to go for, you are unlikely to end up with a cake as tall as the one Portuguese pastry cook Senhor Jose da Palma Revez made for the wedding of his daughter Maria – it stood 81 feet high, and was topped with a replica of a nearby church.)

Rich fruit cakes have become the usual choice of cake for a wedding. Their weight is believed to symbolize fertility. But the symbolism is, for some people, problematic, as a 1987 report from Glasgow University pointed out when it called the cutting of the cake ceremony one of the most potent manifestations of male chauvinism, a clear indication of the loss of the bride's virginity. However, whatever you think of the symbolism, not everyone likes the cake. If you or your partner aren't keen on rich fruit mixtures, why not opt for something different – chocolate, lemon or orange, perhaps – or how about having a different flavour cake on each tier? That way you should cater for everyone else's taste, as well as your own. Or you might consider following the French custom of having a 'Croquembouche', which is a pyramid of choux pastry balls filled with crème patissière and covered with caramel.

You should order your cake at least three months before your wedding, and arrange for it to be delivered to your reception on the morning of the day unless, of course, it's being organized by your hotel or caterer.

DIY receptions

Every trend, so they say, has its backlash, and as wedding receptions have become more and more elaborate over the last decade, so a small but determined band of people have come along with ideas for alternative, non-commercialized wedding parties.

In essence, most people who decide to organize their own reception without specialized help of any kind do so because they feel – and it is easy to see their point of view – that the real identities of brides and bridegrooms tend to get lost under the mass-produced, gimmic-led wedding reception in which personalized balloons and duogrammed serviettes seem to have been gauged more important than atmosphere and people.

Although DIY receptions could very well land you and your family into the role of chefs and party-planners, a less exhausting and by all accounts equally acceptable way of organizing the do would be to ask your guests to bring along the food (and even the booze) themselves. Here's how a reception of this type worked out for one of the couples I spoke to:

We wanted a relaxed, enjoyable time at our wedding, not a do which emphasized formality and expense. We believed very strongly that it would be the people who came along, and not the food and drink, which would provide the atmosphere for the proceedings. We held the reception in the garden of an aunt's house which was near the church, and asked people on the invitations to bring along food and wine. We were a bit worried that we'd get a whole lot of first courses and no puddings, but in the end there was plenty of everything anyone could want. No one seemed to mind that we were asking them to do their own catering – in fact, lots of them seemed to really love the idea. And so many people went to an enormous amount of trouble – we had quite delicious food.

To ensure that the day itself went OK, we organized our friends who said they would be there into groups to set out the food, open the wine and so on. Again, everyone seemed happy to be asked, to be able to play some tangible role in our wedding. It all went brilliantly well.

Sophie and Paul

Present-giving could be a tricky problem if you decide to ask your guests to bring food and wine along to the reception. Obviously buying a present isn't a guest's 'bill' for attending the reception, but you might feel it's a bit much to expect people to cater for themselves and fork out for the prezzie as well. It's probably a good idea to go to considerable lengths to make people feel you really don't expect a gift if you opt for this kind of reception.

If you're very lucky you may find, as Sarah and Martin did, that you have a supply of talented friends who can organize a professional or semi-professional reception for you as their contribution or gift to you on your wedding day.

The party after our wedding was organized totally by us and our friends. Someone we know who owns a pub said he would run the bar for us, and some friends of my mother cooked all the food. A friend who is a baker made the cake. I did most of the flowers myself. A friend of Martin's who is a musician brought his band along to provide the music and – last but certainly not least – someone we know who is a sword-dancer provided the cabaret!

Sarah and Martin

Talking Points

● Discuss between yourselves, and with your families, what kind of memories you would hope your guests will take away from your wedding reception. How would you like them to remember it? What do you hope they will think of it? Use the answers to help you decide what kind of party you want, and where.

• Talk about what sort of occasion you, too, hope your reception will be. Do you think of it very much as a family day, or a chance to chat with your friends? Will the reception you are planning give you plenty of time to talk to everyone you have invited, and if not will you mind?

• Try to work out whether formality really matters to you by deciding how far you're aware of whether things are 'just right' in daily life. Do you mind, for example, if people drop by when you're not expecting it and your flat is a bit of a mess? Do you ever tell people you are called 'Miss Jones', or are you happy for anyone and everyone to call you by your first name? If you're a naturally formal person, the 'etiquette' side of the wedding reception will have some meaning to you. But if formality isn't your style in everyday life, be brave and firm enough to ensure it doesn't take over your wedding day, and make sure those involved with your reception – catering staff, for example – are aware of your wishes.

7

All Dressed Up

And the bride wore . . . a knicker-revealing bright pink mini, a gold lamé trouser suit, a blood-red velvet cape and hood. Or perhaps she went for something a little more traditional . . . a fairytale-inspired feast of antique lace and organza, perhaps, or a cream crinoline with acres of net trailing along behind. The choice of what to wear for your wedding (particularly if you're the female partner) is endless. If you're keen to make a splash, this can be the occasion to let your imagination really run riot – which is why the *haute couture* seasonal shows always end with bridal outfits, Chanel, Christian Lacroix and Christian Dior's *pièces de résistance*.

But you don't, fortunately, have to spend Chanel-style amounts of cash to look a million dollars on your wedding day. And nor do you have to follow someone else's idea of how you should look, if you happen to have very definite opinions on how that might be. What you should do, though, before you head off to the drawing board, the dressmaker's or the shops is sit down and think about what sort of clothes you usually wear and feel comfortable in. Do you like dressing up, or do you tend to spend most of your life slouching round in jeans? Are you a slave to fashion, or are most of your outfits cut along timeless, classic lines? Does your wardrobe contain several sharp, business-like suits, or is it full of Laura Ashley-type flowing dresses? The answers to these questions will help you think about your style, the look you are comfortable in and with, and the look which you would also be wise to follow in your choice of wedding outfit.

Your own style will almost certainly take account of the shape you are, so that what you usually wear will probably also indicate what best flatters your figure and shape. Traditional wedding dresses tend to emphasize one or two aspects of your body: your waist, perhaps, or your arms if the sleeves are a special feature. If you feel unhappy about the way your waist or arms look, try to veer away from these outfits. Don't buy anything which makes you feel ill-at-ease or self-conscious: all eyes will be on you on your wedding day, and there's no point risking feeling fat or over-revealed.

Colour is another aspect to consider before you go to choose your outfit. White, though traditional, is not the ideal colour to go for unless you've got olive-coloured or black skin. English rose, or peaches-and-cream complexions tend to look better in softer, toned whites or ivories, while oyster or pale coffee colours often look great on tanned complexions or naturally golden brown skin. And as well as any of these colours, of course, there's a vast range of other possibilities, from bright red through midnight blue to black. Or, a little more conventionally, you might decide to choose something in a pale colour, or perhaps an understated pattern of stripes or polka dots.

You should also take into account what sort of wedding you are planning when you buy your dress. A Dallas-style dress complete with cathedral train is likely to look a bit out of place if your nuptials are to be celebrated in a small country chapel. If you're marrying in a register office, veils are not usually considered appropriate, although you're quite at liberty to wear a white dress, long or short – one registrar I talked to reckoned that about 30 per cent of brides she married wore one. But a service of blessing after a civil ceremony might not be a suitable place to dress up in the full works, as some vicars get concerned about it being regarded as the actual wedding, which of course it is not.

How to look wonderful without spending a fortune

It's very easy – frighteningly easy – to spend a lot of money on your wedding outfit. After the reception and honeymoon, the bride's attire is likely to form the largest single expense involved in a wedding. And of course if you've got lots of money and are looking to spend a fortune, it's quite possible to spend many thousands on the dress alone – some people spend more on their dress than the average person does on the entire event.

Happily, though, draining your building society account or selling off the family silver isn't the only way to look amazing on your wedding day. With a bit of time and imagination, there's no reason at all why you shouldn't find the dress of your dreams attached to a budget price-tag. Here's how:

● Buy during the sales. Some of the big bridal chains hold annual sales in January and July, and small designer shops sometimes knock down their prices in the late autumn, too. Check your local stores for details of when their next sale is due. In addition, bride's dress 'fairs' are occasionally held at hotels in large towns and cities to sell off end-of-season stock –watch your local press for details of these. Sales are well worth checking out – dresses which originally cost hundreds of pounds can come down to as little as £50 – but, as with all bargain-hunting, don't be seduced into getting something because of the cost alone. Ask yourself whether you'd have been even tempted to buy the dress if it cost £100 more, and if your answer is no you should maybe think again.

● Look in ordinary dress shops and stores as well as in specialized wedding shops. Designers and retailers expect women to spend many hundreds of pounds – far more than they usually would – on their wedding dress, so prices are high. But sometimes, particularly if you're looking for something very simple, or a bit out of the ordinary, you might find an outfit just as suitable, and probably much cheaper, away from the bride's room.

● Buy a secondhand or designer's model dress (these are the dresses the designer makes up for press photographs and to show retailers). Many areas have shops or businesses run from home which specialize in selling secondhand and designer's model dresses – look in the local press and the small ads column of bridal magazines for details. Newspapers and magazines can also put you in touch with individuals trying to find a buyer for their own, recently-worn dress (always ask them to send you a photograph before you trek round to their house to look and try on).

• If you're a whizz on the sewing machine, make your own dress. If you're not, search round for a suitable pattern and material and find a dressmaker who will make it for you. (Butterick and Vogue patterns do a special bridal catalogue which comes complete with a list of dressmakers specializing in bridal wear.)

• Sell your dress after the wedding. This option usually requires a bigger initial outlay than any of the above (although it could, of course, be combined with one of them), but if you can manage to scrape the money together some-how, it's a sensible course of action. After all, what use is a long, white, silk dress going to be to you in the future, not to mention the fact that it's going to be taking up precious wardrobe space for the next 60 years, or going grey in the loft. If you do decide to sell, find a secondhand shop or put an ad in the local paper as soon as you're back from your honeymoon – the more recently-purchased and up-to-date the dress is, the more you can ask for it and the quicker you'll find a buyer.

Accessories

If you're wearing a long dress, your shoes will be mostly out of sight during your wedding day. But whether they're on show or not, choose carefully what to put on your feet. Obviously you'll want to wear stylish and pretty footwear which complements the design of your outfit, but comfort is extremely important, too – you're likely to be walking around quite a lot (including on wet grass, possibly, if you're having pictures taken outside) and may be standing about a good deal, especially if you're having a buffet reception. Buy your shoes well in advance of the day itself, and wear them around the house so they are properly broken in. Alternatively, you might like to consider having a pair of shoes you already own covered or dyed to match your dress – there are several companies which offer this service – again, check the columns of bridal magazines for details, or ask the assistant at a bridal boutique in your area if she knows of anyone who could do it.

Finding the right underwear is important, too. There are plenty of designers around who make beautiful silk and satin lingerie, and many women who would never usually spend so much on a bra or knickers find themselves being persuaded to splash out for their wedding day trousseau. If you can afford it and having silk undies makes you feel good, fine. But don't be seduced into parting with lots of cash if you'd feel just as comfortable in some underwear you've already got – you'd do better putting the money towards buying a slightly better veil or shoes. And make sure that you're not in any danger of having a bra strap peeping out of your dress on your wedding pictures, or a knicker line spoiling the look of your stretchtight skirt.

Veils and headdresses have long been an essential element in bridal get-up, and the majority of brides continue to wear something, usually flowers, often a veil and occasionally a hat, on their head. Your headgear needs to match your dress in terms of style as well as colour, length and fabric. Veils come in a wide variety of types, from extremely intricate, beaded creations to a plain net. You shouldn't try to economize by buying a cheap nylon veil to wear over a silk dress, even if you're only wearing the veil to walk up the aisle and intend to remove it for the reception – the inferior quality will, unfortunately, show.

Tradition dictates that brides should arrive at the ceremony with their veils covering their faces, and then lift them either when they reach the altar or when they sign the register. It is, however, quite acceptable to wear your veil back from your face throughout, and your decision on what to do might depend to some extent on the type of headdress you plan to wear, and how your hair is to be done. Try out different hairstyles at home or at the hairdresser's, and when you're happy with your hair, work out how your headgear would best complement it.

Something old, something new

Many brides like to follow the old tradition of wearing items which are old, new, borrowed and blue, in keeping with the old verse which dictates that bridal attire should include:

Something old, something new
Something borrowed, anything blue.
Something given by another,
Luckiest if the gift of lover.

The rhyme is about symbolism as well as superstition: something old so she will keep some of the love of her family and friends in her new life; something new to signify the success which will be hers in the future; something blue as an emblem of constancy and loyalty; and something borrowed so friends will be ever-generous when she needs them.

The rhyme is not the definitive statement on what the lucky bride should be wearing as she sets out to the church, however. Superstition surrounds the whole issue of bridal outfits; amongst other things, it is said to be unlucky for the bride to see herself in her complete costume before leaving for the ceremony, and some people believe the final stitches should not be put into the wedding gown until the last possible minute (a little difficult to organize in these days of off-the-peg styles, that one). The colour of the wedding dress was traditionally thought to be significant too: white, silver, pink and gold were all considered lucky colours, while blue signified constancy and green danger.

Top tips on how to look good

Here's some advice from Missie Graves, co-owner of the leading London bridal boutique Tatters, on how to go about putting together a winning look for your wedding day.

In a way, it's best not to be too set on what you want before you go to the shops. People who have a very definite idea of what they want often can't find it. It's OK to have a picture of how you'd like to look in your mind, but don't stick too rigidly to the details of it. If you are quite determined to have a particular look you could, of course, go along to a designer and ask her to make it up, but you've got to be able to trust the designer, and for that reason I'd advise going along to someone who's already made a dress for you in the past, if at all possible.

Likewise if you buy from a shop, you've got to be prepared to trust the people who run it when they give you advice on how to wear it, what you might wear with it and so on.

When you try a dress on, ask yourself how comfortable you feel, and whether it instills confidence in you. You shouldn't be overawed by your wedding dress, and it shouldn't take you over or engulf your personality. You should be wearing the dress, not it wearing you. And you should also enjoy it and be in love with it.

As far as colours are concerned there aren't many hard and fast rules, although very pale people should wear an ivory or pale pink dress rather than a white one. As far as styles are concerned, bear in mind that simple dresses are sophisticated, and often harder to wear than more fussy, frilly designs.

You don't have to spend a lot of money to look good. One-off dresses often cost large amounts of money, but a much cheaper dress can look just as good. For a few women it's really important to wear something completely original, but for the majority looking good is all that counts and, after all, there's only going to be one bride at your wedding so you shouldn't find anyone else there wearing the same outfit!

Hair and make-up

Make sure you think about how you would like to wear your hair well in advance, as you might want to try out several different styles before finding one which you feel really comfortable with and which seems to suit your dress.

As far as both hair and make-up are concerned, the main rule is not to metamorphose into another person by going for a style and look which is totally different from usual. Obviously, you want to look special on your wedding day – but don't go over the top. As with your outfit, the best idea is to start with the way you usually look and enhance it. Let your hairdresser (and make-up artist if you're having your make-up applied professionally) see you as you are normally, and explain that you want to appear striking, but not unrecognizable, on your wedding day.

If you're putting on your own make-up, have plenty of practice runs and apply it with time to spare on the day itself so you've got time to start again if it all goes wrong. Here are a few other general points to bear in mind:

—Make sure your foundation is the same colour as your skin or a shade darker, as anything lighter will make you look washed out in the photographs.

—Don't apply too heavy a foundation, as it may appear orange on the photographs.

—Keep blusher soft and understated: you're likely to warm up quickly on the day and will appear flushed if you're wearing too much blusher.

Menswear

The choice of what to wear for the bridegroom is, of course, a much more limited one than for his bride. Basically, he must decide whether to go for the formal morning suit, or a lounge suit. Scots, though, may want to wear their clan tartan in a kilt, and men in the forces often wear their uniforms to get married. Most men who go for a lounge suit wear one which belongs to them (many see the occasion as an excellent excuse to invest in a new suit), but they can also be hired. Wearing a morning suit almost always involves hiring, and there are several specialist companies which provide this service – look under 'Men's Wear Hire' in the Yellow Pages. There are several styles and colours for morning dress; the Edwardian look, with a black and grey morning suit, and winged collar shirt worn with a cravat, has become increasingly fashionable in recent years. Patterned waistcoats are quite popular, and add a dash of originality and colour, although you'll probably have to buy your own as many hire companies only stock the traditional grey or black. Most men who decide to wear morning dress hire a top hat too, although there's no need to actually put it on at any point.

The bridegroom sets the dress code for all the main men involved in the wedding ceremony, so if he's in morning suit the best man, the two fathers, and the ushers should be as well. Traditionally, all wear buttonholes which should be provided by the bridegroom.

Talking Points

● How important to you is the way you look? Does your partner give similar weight to his appearance? If clothes matter more to one of you than the other, do you think it might cause any problems in the future?

● What, if anything, would you like to change about your partner's appearance? What would he like to change about yours? Hopefully, the answer in both cases will be not a lot. It's crucially important not to nurse secretly ideas of transforming your partner either in character or in his sense of style, after you're married. *Don't* assume he'll change, even if he says he will. People do, inevitably, influence one another's tastes, but this is a very gradual, slow process. And don't forget that he's as likely to alter your tastes as you are to change his!

● Do you both like shopping, or does one of you enjoy it more than the other? Who will do the weekly shop in your house after your marriage? You don't, of course, have to decide rigidly who is going to do which domestic chores before you marry, but it is worth talking generally about what each expects of the other – you may find one or both of you is making unrealistic assumptions.

8

The Price of Love

Love and marriage may or may not go together like the horse and carriage in the old song, but money and marriage inevitably do. Seen in the most mercenary terms, marriage may be about little more than finances – though, thankfully, unions based on purely mercantile considerations seem to be more plentiful in history and less common in modern times. But however romantic the partnership, however impractical the couple, in every marriage there will come a point when money will raise its ugly head. How that moment affects your partnership depends, to a very large extent, on how aware the two of you are of the economic realities of life, and on the thought and preparation you have given to the thorny subject of finances.

Paying for the wedding

For most couples, money becomes an issue to be reckoned with from the moment they decide to get married. The cost of a wedding, never to be sniffed at, has in recent times rocketed. A survey in the magazine Wedding and Home in 1990 found that the average price had gone up by a whopping 25 per cent on the previous year. (Although one of the most expensive weddings in history was in fact back in 1981 when the wedding of a sheik's son and a princess saw 20,000 guests entertained for a week at a cost of £22 million.)

Traditionally, as everyone knows, the cost of a wedding was borne by the bride's father with a few sundry items met by the bridegroom, but increasingly these days the tide is turning. Sometimes this is because where a couple are in their thirties or even older, it seems unfair and overburdensome to expect elderly parents to foot the bill for a big bash. In other cases, couples feel too guilty about allowing their parents to fork out all the cash required to realize their dreams. And sometimes couples decide to take over responsibility for the entire budget themselves in order to retain control of their wedding, fearing that whoever controls the purse strings will also call the wedding tune.

> We decided at the very beginning that we were going to pay for everything ourselves, and told both sets of parents of our decision. We knew we wouldn't be able to afford to spend a lot of money on it, but we felt very strongly that remaining in charge was the more important consideration. We wanted to organize our wedding our way, without outside interference.
>
> *Sophie*

There's no doubt that paying for the wedding yourself is probably going to mean more clout for you and your partner in drawing up the plans for the ceremony and the reception afterwards. However, for many couples footing the entire bill is quite impossible, and in any case many fathers have spent a lifetime saving up for this very moment. If this is your situation, the best way to proceed is probably to sit down with the bride's parents, draw up a list of items which will need paying for, and sort out how much is available for each and from whom.

By far the largest item on your list will be the reception, or wedding party, which is likely to account for at least a fifth of the entire budget, with only the honeymoon ranking near it in amount. Included in reception costs are the catering and food charges, which will eat up the biggest portion of your funds, the drinks, the cake, the hire of a hall or party room, and a second or evening party, if you are holding one. These costs are the ones most usually paid for by the bride's parents. You might want to suggest helping pay for some part of them yourself, but do be careful to be sensitive in making your offer.

If you do feel, for whatever reason, that you would like to make some contribution to the costs involved in your wedding, it might be easier to look at the costs involved in the second main item list, that of the charges surrounding the ceremony. Bridegrooms traditionally pay the costs of the actual service, but this is usually the smallest item of a catalogue which also includes the invitations and stationery, photography and video, and flowers, and the transport. These charges, too, should in theory be paid by the bride's parents, but in many cases either the couple themselves or the bridegroom's parents may undertake to cover some of them.

Dressing up to the nines doesn't come cheap: the cost of the bridal couple's outfits, the attendants' clothes and going-away suits accounts for roughly another fifth of the entire wedding budget. Again, tradition has always dictated that the costs of the bride's attire is paid for by her father, but these days it is very common for the bride to pay for her own dress and for the bridegroom to foot the bill for his suit or hired morning dress. A more vexed question surrounds the cost of the attendants' clothes, and whether these are paid for by the bride, her father, or the individuals themselves. There isn't a hard and fast rule, but it's important to reach an agreement fairly early on in the proceedings, so everyone knows where they stand. In general, if you are determined to dictate the style, fabric and colour of the bridesmaids' dresses, it would seem to be only fair that you also pay for them; if, on the other hand, you are allowing your attendants a free or fairly free rein, they are quite likely to be prepared to pay all or part of the cost themselves.

Wedding insurance

It's making a big hole in your parents' life savings and no small dent in your own and your partner's finances, and if anything went wrong it would be nigh on impossible to arrange and pay for another event on the same scale. So it only makes sense, really, to shell out another few pounds on taking out an insurance policy to cover unforeseen disasters on your wedding day. In the unlikely event of anything happening to throw a spanner in the works, your policy will at least stem a financial as well as emotional disaster resulting from your ruined day.

Several insurance companies have packages which under-write damage to bridal attire, presents and photographs, as well as other risks including a cancelled ceremony resulting from the ill-health of one of the principal players. Few if any policies will, though, cushion you from the blow of your loved one pulling out at the eleventh hour – a change of heart by one of the two main parties is almost always excluded in the small print.

Present lists

Unless you are asking your guests to do the catering themselves and bring food and drink with them to the reception (see Chapter 6 for more information if you want a DIY party of this type), your guests will expect and be expected to provide you and your partner with a gift which, traditionally, should be of use to you in your marital home. In the past, this automatically meant that couples, most of whom were living with their parents up to the point of marriage, were kitted out with toasters, frying pans, fridges and sofas. But times have changed, and these days most individuals getting married have lived some kind of independent life away from their families before getting engaged. More and more often they are already living with their partner at the time of their engagement, or living separately in their own flats or houses. All of which has rather turned on its head the old idea of marriage as a time to buy a new home and furnish it; these days couples are quite likely to be looking to put one of their two houses or flats on the market, and to sell off their spare sets of pots and pans in the secondhand column of their local newspaper!

But whether you're hoping to reap the traditional gifts or add to your collection of art deco vases, help is at hand in the form of a vast array of shops and stores of all sizes and in towns and cities throughout the country which are just longing to help you ensure you receive the gifts you want. You can, of course, organize your own present list without any help from anyone; but, be warned, such a task requires time and patience and is likely to take a fairly hefty toll on your shoe leather. As well as trudging round any number of shops and noting down the precise details of the items you require (make, design, price, colour, quantity required, where available), you and/or your partner and parents and parents-in-law will have to be willing to field telephone enquiries from guests on what to buy, as well as scrupulously recording and circulating details of which items are already spoken for.

Not surprisingly, more and more couples are turning to the less time-consuming device of placing a list at a department store near their home. Almost all towns now have at least one store which offers this service (usually known as the 'Bride's Book' or 'Bridal List'), many computerized. In most cases you will be given a sheet or booklet with ideas and suggestions of items you may need (don't be daunted or carried away by these – they're only prompts), and invited to wander round the different departments for a couple of hours or more ticking off the things you would like to include on your list, (in posher stores you may also be offered the assistance of a 'bridal adviser' to accompany you on your tour). Try to choose a day other than a Saturday if you can to compile your list, to avoid having to battle through hordes of weekend shoppers. And don't worry about ending up with a seemingly endless list, as your guests will appreciate having plenty of gifts to choose from; similarly, they will want to have some choice about how much they spend, so make sure you have items which cost varying amounts. But you're not being cheeky if you decide to include a few fairly major pieces of equipment, such as a washing machine or dining-room table, on your list – you may find that a group of old college friends may decide to club together to buy them for you.

A shop list has all sorts of advantages, not least the fact that it virtually eliminates the possibility of being bought two of anything you wanted only one of. Even if someone manages to slip through the net and duplicate something (as one of my friends did when she phoned up the store, asked what was on the list and then bought me a casserole dish independently of the 'Bride's Book' department, without realizing that would by-pass the system), you will almost certainly find the shop is willing to exchange it for you. A shop list is also easier for busy friends and relatives, in that they are not obliged to spend their precious shopping hours searching round for sheets which are exactly the right shade of peach to match your curtains (usually, they can order by credit card over the phone, by cheque through the post, or in person by visiting the store). Guests are also spared the worry of how to transport your dozen wine glasses or cut glass vase to your door, and are excused the task of having to wrap your presents up (most stores deliver purchased gifts from your list gift-wrapped, although it does seem rather unnecessarily wasteful to do so, and you might want to tell them not to bother).

Another advantage of a store list might be that the shop will hold all your presents and deliver them en masse, possibly waiting until you are back from your honeymoon. However, this is not always the policy, and you may find as I did that they want to send a van round every week for weeks on end delivering the goods your guests have most recently purchased for you. Ensuring you are at home at the same time each week can prove annoying and frustrating, not to say quite impossible when you're actually away on your honeymoon, so make sure you check the full details of the shop's service before you choose it for your list.

Some couples find one shop just isn't big enough to stock all the gift deas they're hoping to harvest from their wedding guests. This problem can be solved by having, as the Prince and Princess of Wales did, lists at not just one but *two* stores. Or, if you're really keen to shop around but can't face the task of organizing and running your own list, there are companies which will act as a clearing-house, liaising on your behalf with both your guests and the shops you have chosen gifts from.

If you're particularly well-endowed with the cheaper things which go to make up a home, you might prefer to ask your family and friends to pay some money into a bank, building society or store account, so that you build up a sizable (you hope) amount of cash which you can then use for a just one or two really expensive items. This idea is much more common-place on the continent than in Britain – here, many people seem to find the idea of giving money as a wedding present rather distasteful. However, there is no reason why this should be so, and any relatives and friends worth having will be happy to know they are helping you buy something useful for you in your life together.

Organizing your finances after the honeymoon

Complex, time-consuming and difficult though the financial side of a wedding may be, its trickiness pales in comparison with the problems of organizing your joint affairs once the day itself ends and the marriage begins. No marriage, however well-cushioned, however high-class, can exist in a bubble unpenetrated by economic considerations. Money matters, in a love affair as elsewhere; and if it doesn't seem too pressing a concern in the immediate future, you should spare a few minutes together to try to imagine how financial factors will affect you in a few years' time when you've got a couple of toddlers, a mammoth mortgage and (albeit, perhaps, temporarily) only one income.

To encourage couples to think about how they will run their economic affairs in married life, some financial advisers suggest you should draw up a marriage contract, a document which provides a sort of framework or set of guidelines for how you intend to organize your bank account(s), pay off your mortgage, and buy your food. They can also make clear which items in the household and assets in the bank belong to you individually and which are owned jointly. At present in Britain marriage contracts have no legal standing, so you can't sue your partner for reneging on the deal. Marriage contracts can, of course, cover any and every area of nuptial life, not merely the economic side, and can also lay down ground rules for how you will proceed in the event of serious disagreements – you may want to make a pact, for example, that neither of you will consider filing for divorce before consulting a marriage guidance counsellor.

Though widely used on the continent and in America, marriage contracts haven't really taken off in Britain – many people seem to regard them as too formal and unromantic. However, the principle of setting aside a bit of time to sort out who is going to pay for what is still a good one. Some important questions to consider are:

—Whether to carry on running separate bank and/or building society accounts, or to pay both your salaries into one joint account, or whether to keep your separate accounts but open a joint account for household expenses. Some couples like to do away with separate accounts as holding all their money 'in common' seems to them to be an essential ingredient of married life, while for others keeping their financial affairs apart is an important way of retaining their status as individuals. Many couples find keeping their own accounts and opening a joint account is the ideal solution.

—How to divide up the household expenses. Are you going to pay half each, or does one of you earn more than the other so that a straight half-share would be unfair? If you are going to divide your expenses according to means, how will you work out how much to pay?

—How you are going to save for holidays, a new car, your next home. Will one of you take on the responsibility of saving up because s/he pays less of the running expenses, or will you decide to each save a set amount each month? If you agree to each save an amount each month, ask yourselves how you would feel if the other partner failed, for whatever reason, to bank his/her amount.

—What you're each going to call yourselves after your marriage. Most couples still follow convention by changing the wife's surname to that of her husband, but a growing band of women feel that getting married shouldn't have to mean losing your identity as an individual, and that holding on to one's pre-marriage name is an important element in this. Others feel equally strongly that adopting the same name is an essential part of creating a new family unit.

Basically, you have three choices as far as names are concerned.

1.   Change the wife's surname to that of her husband (or, if for any reason it makes more sense, change the husband's surname to that of his wife). Make sure you tell your bank (they will have to issue you with new cheque books, and you will probably be given a new account number); your building society; the DVLC at Swansea if you hold a driving licence; your doctor's surgery; your dentist; and the passport office. Make sure you inform these people well before your wedding, especially the passport office if you are intending to honeymoon abroad and wish to travel under your new name.

2.   Each keep your own surname. This is (in my experience, at least) not too difficult, although you will find that some relatives and friends insist on addressing post to you in your husband's name, however clear you have made your wishes. However, anyone you really care about will almost certainly respect your choice, even if they themselves find it strange. A few may try to deter you by suggesting that not changing your name is disloyal to your husband, eccentric or even illegal. Don't listen to any of them: keeping your own name is a statement of how you see your independence within your married relationship, and is perfectly within your rights. Be prepared, though, for some battles: I have had many tustles with officials at the Inland Revenue who for several months after my marriage insisted on sending bills to me as Mrs Smith. I didn't pay any of them, laughed out loud when the inspector told me I had to produce a deed poll if I intended to call myself by my birth name, and won in the end. However, I'm well aware that the arrival of children could cause headaches when it comes to what to call them: whose surname should they be given, or ought they to be given a double-barrelled version of both?

3. Use one surname professionally and another for your private life. In practice, this almost always means the female partner using her so-called maiden name at work, and her husband's name for everything else. Depending on how you see it, the split personality this option results in can lead to either mammoth muddles, or a clear-cut divide between work and home in your life. For many women, this way of overcoming the problem of what to call yourself after marriage proves extremely successful – but be aware, before you decide to go ahead, that many women find that juggling two names is just too much hassle. If you decide to try it, you will find your bank happy to let you have two accounts, one in each name, although you might be asked to produce your marriage certificate to prove you are who you say you are – banks are sometimes suspicious of people who want multiple accounts, as it could be a way of defrauding the tax inspector. You should also be careful that any airline tickets are booked in the name on your passport, otherwise you will need to go on your holiday or business trip armed with official documents proving who you are.

Useful Address
The British Insurance and Investment Brokers Association, BIIBA House, 14 Bevis Marks, London EC3A 7NT. (Will provide you with a list of local insurance brokers to contact for information about companies which provide a 'wedding insurance' package.)

9
Ever After

Driving off into the sunset together after your reception (him, depressingly, still almost always at the wheel) is, of course, only the start. The wedding may be over, with the photographer's snaps and the top tier of the cake the only legacy of your 18 months of careful planning, but the marriage, the reason for it all, is about to begin.

But will it work out? Or, to be more exact, *how* will it work out? Are you on the road to 40, 50 or even 60 years of wedded bliss, or en route to bolstering the ever-spiralling statistics which already rate your chances of divorce as high as one in three?

The simple answer is, of course, that you don't, and can't, know what lies ahead. Indeed, putting your trust in one another, the winds of fortune and/or God is very much what marriage is about. As the vows imply, future physical health, material wealth and worldly success are unknown quantities for you and your partner as you walk down the aisle together. All you can be fairly sure of, in fact, is that you'll have to face difficult times as well as good ones.

But acknowledging that the future is impossible to read doesn't mean we don't have a role in shaping it – or, to be more precise, in shaping our response to the events which will come our way. We cannot protect ourselves and our relationships from the ravages and realities of the world (and nor would we want to); but we can work to build up a partnership which has a fair chance of withstanding the trials and tribulations which will inevitably come its way.

According to the experts, the first couple of years are particularly vital in creating a viable marriage. The root causes of many divorces, even those which take place many years after the wedding, can frequently be traced back to those initial 24 months. So it's important to be aware that your early days together will 'set the scene' for your marriage for many years to come, and consequently you should be prepared to put some time and trouble into ensuring that things go well. Be aware, too, that some factors could mean you're more at risk of encountering difficulties: if you're expecting a baby when you get married, or if you're still in your teens, or if your parents or your partner's object to the union, statistics show that problems could be more likely to come your way. But don't despair if you do fall into one of these categories: there are plenty of examples of happy marriages which have survived despite appearing to have the cards stacked against them.

Whatever you've got going for you or ranged against you statistically, however, one thing is quite certain: if you and your partner don't communicate properly, your marriage is doomed. Communication is *the* key ingredient in making your relationship work. Now the chances are that, at the moment anyway, you and your partner manage to communicate extremely well. You spend a lot of time talking to one another, discussing your wedding preparations and making plans. You probably find plenty of space and time for cuddling and making love, too. You're close: you've got a fairly good idea of what your partner is thinking and feeling, and you're confident he or she knows quite a lot about you, too.

All of which is, of course, a good and sound basis for putting together a healthy marriage. The trouble is, though, that even couples who find communicating easy before they get married sometimes discover that a bit more effort is required after the wedding to maintain the same level of knowledge and intimacy. Whereas before your wedding you probably set aside time to go out together or be alone together, it's all too easy after the wedding to fall into the trap of thinking that because you've settled and sealed your relationship, it doesn't need nurturing in the same way any more. Equally, many couples think that because they're now permanently together they'll inevitably get time to themselves without having to create it. This may or may not have been true in the past, but it certainly isn't isn't true for many of us today. Busy lives, crowded diaries, demanding careers, the pressures of keeping up other friendships independently of our partners, mean the time and space essential to maintaining a good marriage can go by the board unless we guard it fiercely. Always be aware of how much time you and your partner are spending together: and don't be tricked into thinking that merely because you fall into the same bed each night, you're necessarily seeing enough of one another. I loathe the term 'quality time' because it can make us forget that life isn't perfect, we have to listen to and care for our partners through their difficult moments as well as their good ones (and, of course, it's often during the *hardest* times that growth in a relationship occurs). Yet I have to admit that it's no good expecting your marriage to survive well if you don't ensure that you sometimes give of your best to your partner. In other words, it's no good only giving each other those moments when you're completely exhausted at the end of a busy day, or when you're preoccupied with some problem at work, or when you're tense and fretful. Make sure you earmark some hours to spend together when you know you'll be on top of things, even if this should mean missing a Saturday night out with your friends, or a Sunday lunch with your parents.

But time together, whatever mood you're in, is only useful if you're prepared to really listen to one another. Don't assume that you know each other so well that words don't matter. There will be ways, of course, in which you do know what the other is thinking, but people change and it's important to keep talking about ideas, everyday events, and issues you care about.

Communicating also means getting to know as much as possible about your partner's background and childhood. This is important because it helps you realize why he or she holds certain beliefs or has certain habits, but also because it can help prevent misunderstandings which, over time, can damage your relationship. Childhood experiences confer assumptions which, even in the cold, logical light of adulthood, we find hard to shake off. To take but one example: my father has always, from my earliest memories, got up at 7.30 am to make my mother a cup of tea to drink in bed. The result is that I associate early morning tea-making with chivalrous men, and always expected that the man I married would get up half an hour before me to bring me a cup of tea. Sadly, my dreams came to nothing: not because my husband isn't a kind-hearted, chivalrous man, but because in his family it was his mother who made the early-morning tea. So in those early months while I was wondering at 7.30 am each day why he had turned out to be less than perfect, he too was lying there wondering why I wasn't as good a wife as his mother had been. It's all down to conditioning, and if you find your conditioning is at loggerheads you have to acknowledge the fact and try to draw up a new scheme which suits you both. Nowadays, we take it in turns to make the early morning tea.

Marriage after living together

If you've been living together in the months or years before you get married (and statistics show that you're more and more likely to have done so), you might assume that life after the wedding will continue much as it was before. Surprisingly, this only seems to turn out to be true for a minority of couples. For most, signing a wedding certificate somehow changes the relationship. It's not necessarily better or worse after marriage, but it's indisputably different.

I hadn't expected the wedding to change anything, but after it I felt increasingly trapped in my relationship. Before, when we were just living together, we tolerated each other's ways more, but after marriage I think we became aware that living with one another's tiresome habits wasn't just something to put up with for a few years, it was for ever. That was quite frightening for a time.

Another thing which surprised and scared me was that I found myself slipping into traditional 'female' roles in the house which I just hadn't in the past. I was spending more and more time in the kitchen, and the responsibility for keeping it tidy and cooking the meals seemed to come down more and more to me. I suddenly started to see myself becoming a mother, acting like a homemaker, although we were still both working outside the home. In the end we talked about it and I resolved to fight it, but it's not been easy.

Amanda, 35

Dealing with conflict

Conflict is both inevitable and healthy in a marriage. Inevitable because it's simply not possible for two individuals, with different ideas, different backgrounds, different points of view, to live together without occasionally finding themselves in dispute, and healthy because dealing with conflict when it arises is how relationships mature.

But dealing with disputes in the first months of marriage can be a scary business, because we're unsure of how far we can push each other and afraid of the anger we might unleash. Yet at the same time these early arguments are also a sign of the liberating nature of marriage: they make us aware that we are able to row without jeopardizing our relationship. 'I came to realize that we could have arguments, even really heated ones, and yet still be safe together', explains Amanda. This lesson is an important one, as it gives couples a licence to take note of problems when they arise, rather than ignoring them, which is a bigger danger in the long run.

However, being aware of the overall benefits of occasionally falling out won't necessarily help you through the thick of a slanging match. To argue positively, it's worth bearing in mind a few basic ground-rules.

—Choose to sort out a problem that's worrying you at a time when you don't expect to be interrupted or disturbed.

It's not a good idea, for example, to launch into a critique of his smoking habit five minutes before friends come round for a dinner party. You'll only succeed in opening a wound which will quietly fester all evening, spoiling your dinner party and lessening your chances of ever sorting out your grievance.

—Try not to conduct an argument by raining down accusations and criticisms of your partner's behaviour and character. Instead, explain why you think something is wrong from your own point of view – as in 'I feel we don't spend enough time together in the evenings because you're often at the pub', rather than the simpler and cruder version: 'You're always at the pub'. Making accusations of this sort will in all probability only lead to him accusing you of something similar ('So what? You're always at your mother's') rather than discussing the problem you want to raise.

—Aim to keep your comments to one theme. Try not to get sidetracked into discussing other areas of your life, especially not past disputes – they have a habit of creeping back into any new argument, where they only serve to harbour resentment.

—Think of yourself as negotiating with your partner when you find yourselves in dispute. A mature relationship is not about winning and losing when problems present themselves, but resolving a difficult situation so that you both gain.

Happy families

Getting married is an acknowledgement of the fact that our partner and our relationship has moved into centre-stage in our life, and that from this time on our strongest bond and first loyalty is to husband or wife. Yet our first family, the family in which we grew up, does not cease to be important: it may have been inevitably downgraded by virtue of our marriage, but it retains an undeniable stake in our affections.

During the early months of marriage, some people find it difficult to work out what role their parents now play in their lives. They wonder whether they should see so much of their parents, and whether they should share information with their parents in the same way they have done in the past. Sometimes these initial 'split loyalties' may lead to misunderstandings between partners: a husband whose wife insists on continuing to spend each Saturday afternoon with her mother may wonder how he is falling short, not realizing that his partner's visits are about her relationship with her mother, and nothing to do with supposed failings on his part. To prevent such misunderstandings it's vital to talk together about your two sets of parents, and to recognize together the importance they have in your life and the ways in which they will continue to play an important part. You shouldn't try to shut your parents or in-laws out of your lives, but equally you should beware of them being too dominant a force in your relationship.

It's often difficult, at least initially, to cope with some aspects of your partner's parents' life: you may find some of their demands on your husband or wife unreasonable, or you may find their habits or way of doing things odd or amusing. Beware, though, of over-criticizing or making fun of your partner's family to him; even if he agrees with much of what you say, he will eventually become defensive of his roots, and will take their side against you. Instead, try to accept your partner's family for the people they are. Try not to spend the whole time comparing and contrasting them with your own parents, and be aware of the fact that just as you find some of their ways strange, so they probably find you a little odd.

Just as it's not a good idea to criticize your partner's family too much for fear of dividing his loyalties, so it's unwise to go on about his failings in front of them. Instead, work at presenting yourselves as a united couple: talk about the things you're planning together, and the shared life you've worked out for yourselves.

If your parents-in-law are overdemanding and appear to want too big a role in organizing your lives, talk honestly to your partner about it. Try not to wade in with a tirade of negative insults directed against his family, though. Acknowledge that some of the problem might be your fault, but point out that you feel your relationship is suffering because you're not spending enough time together, or because the decisions you should be making together are being taken out of your hands.

Try to explain your feelings to your in-laws together, and as honestly as possible. Be positive about it: tell them that you have to learn to make decisions for yourselves, and that being a married couple means taking responsibility yourselves for certain areas of your life. Assert your rights to privacy, time alone together and freedom to do what you want. Don't accept, either, any argument from them that their wider experience means they can make 'better' decisions than you can; point out that we all have the right to make our own mistakes in life, and that it is only through making mistakes that we learn for the future.

Married sex

In the past, a couple's sex life started from their marriage: these days, so the wag would say, it very often ends with it. Yet, while there's no doubt that for many couples sex is different after the wedding, the change is nothing like as significant as some would have you believe. Basically, if sex was good before you were married, there's every likelihood that it will continue to be good afterwards; equally, if it wasn't all it could have been beforehand, don't expect walking down the aisle to work a miracle.

I don't think marriage has affected our sex life in any major way. We certainly didn't stop making love as often – in fact, I think we probably have sex more often these days than we did when we were engaged. What I will admit, though, is that a bit of the excitement and naughtiness has gone out of it – that feeling that you were doing something you really shouldn't have been doing. But on the plus side, sex seems a deeper, more mature expression of our love than it used to be.

Clare, 30; married three years

Sex, like everything else in marriage, depends on good communication. In an ideal world, communicating to your partner about what you like and don't like while making love would, perhaps, be unnecessary, just as saying what they want always seems to be unnecessary for those airport novel heroines when they meet the man of their dreams and fall into bed with him. The real world, however, tends to need more explanations, and even if explaining your feelings and needs is sometimes difficult, it's worth doing. It's no good keeping silent and hoping against hope that your partner will one day stumble upon the touch or caress you've been longing for: tell him (or her) that there are other things you'd like to try, and ask what he (or she) wants, too. Variety will keep your sex life alive and interesting.

Although marriage theoretically means more opportunities for making love, some couples find that, precisely because it's always available, they make love less often, or not as often as they would like. This seems especially true of couples where each partner has a busy, demanding life; as a friend said to me recently, if even one of you is lively enough to get things going, the other – though tired – may liven up. But if you're both completely exhausted by the time you crawl into bed at night, sex really doesn't get a look in. If you find your sex life suffering from perpetual tiredness, try to make time for one another at weekends. Don't fall into the trap, either, of thinking sex isn't worthwhile unless you have intercourse: sometimes making love in other ways can be just as satisfying for both of you.

What to aim for

A healthy marriage is about caring for one another – healing one another from the hurts of life, encouraging one another into new pastures and along new paths, and being strong for one another when the going gets tough. It's also, and this can sometimes be difficult, about recognizing that the worries, concerns, triumphs and successes of our partner's life matter as much as those of our own.

A healthy marriage is always changing, and hopefully most of the time it's actually improving. But change and improvement don't happen on their own: marriage, like so much of life, requires commitment and, at least some of the time, hard work. If you're prepared to invest that into your relationship, you really should be able to look back on your wedding day as the most important day of your life.

What is important to you?

Sharing one another's interests and concerns, and respecting one another's values, are an essential part of a good relationship. The following exercise may help you think about how much you have in common, and about which areas of your lives could produce possible conflicts in the years ahead.

Make two copies of the following list, and give one to your partner. Each of you should then look through the list and mark with a tick the importance you attach to the attribute mentioned. Then, go back through the list and mark with a cross what you think your partner's attitude is to the things mentioned.

When both of you have completed your lists, compare them. If on one person's chart the cross and tick are very far apart, that partner perceives, rightly or wrongly, a difference in your attitudes to some part of your life, and you should talk together about whether he or she is right and whether you should do anything about it. Equally, if the tick on one chart is very far from the cross on another chart, you also have something to discuss.

Talk openly and honestly to one another about the way you answered the questions. Ask yourselves if any of the answers your partner gave surprised you. If you discover that there is some area of your life in which your values are very different, acknowledge that it is an area which you still need to talk through.

	Very	Fairly	Not very	Not at all
Being tidy and well-organized				
Good food				
Being punctual				
Reading				
Football				
Going out regularly				
My own friends				
Family ties				
Inviting people home				
Having time to myself				
Showing affection				
Saying 'I love you'				
Talking together regularly				
Keeping the peace				
Getting my own way				
Honesty				
Keeping promises				
Going to church				
Keeping to a strict budget				
Buying surprise presents				
Saving				
Making careful decisions				
My job				
Promotion				
Living in this area				

Talking Points

- **In** your parents' marriage, who:

    - cooked the meals?
    - took care of the car?
    - paid the bills?
    - did the washing-up?
    - made early morning tea?
    - did the shopping?
    - decorated the house?

Note down the answers to these questions, and ask your partner to do the same. Compare your answers, and talk about what they mean for the expectations you bring to your own marriage.

- Show your partner as many photographs as you can find of your family and yourself in your early years. Share with him your memories of family holidays, family fun and important events of your childhood.

Useful Addresses
Relate (formerly the National Marriage Guidance Council), Herbert Gray College, Little Church Street, Rugby CV21 3AP. Provides information on pre-marital courses and marital counselling.

The Catholic Marriage Advisory Council (address at the end of Chapter 3) also provides counselling, to non-Catholic couples as well as Catholic ones.

Index

abroad, marrying 55–7
Anglican Church 24–5, 33–8;
    proportion of weddings in 10;
    qualifications for marrying in
    34–5; wedding service in 36–7
announcement of engagement
    12–15

banns 24–5
best man 52–3
best woman 54–5
blessing, service of 35; outfit for
    79
bridesmaids 53–4; cost of outfits
    89

cake, wedding 70, 74–5
caterers 68–9
Catholic Church, *see* Roman
    Catholic
children, at wedding 72–3; as
    attendants 54
church, wedding in a 21–4, 29–
    41; feelings about 9–11; *see
    also* Anglican, Roman
    Catholic, Methodist
costs of the wedding and who
    pays 87–9

dress, bride's 78–81; cost of 89
drinks (at the reception) 73–4

fees: Anglican Church 38

guests: at a register office 47; *see
    also* invitations

hair, bride's 84–5
hotel, reception at 69–71

humanist ceremony 11, 23, 48–52

in-laws 102–4; role after the
    wedding 102–4
insurance, wedding 89–90
invitations 71–3

Jewish wedding 41–3; as
    proportion of all weddings 10

legal requirements 24–7
living together 35, 100–1

make-up 84–5
marriage: reasons for 7–9;
    feelings about 9–12; legal
    meaning of 12; contract 93–4
Methodist Church 38; proportion
    of weddings in 10
money 87–96; saving on 79–81,
    75–6; *see also* costs
music during service 32–3

names, changing of or keeping
    your own 95–6

parents: significance of wedding
    for 63, 71; role in the
    ceremony 31; not taking over
    72; role after the wedding
    102–4
photographs 58–62;
    photographer's packages 60; at
    a register office 46; time for
    58, 61–2
preparation, pre-marriage: in the
    Anglican Church 35–7; in the
    Catholic Church 39–40; in the
    Jewish faith 42–3

presents 90–3; if planning a DIY reception 76
press, announcements in the 13–15

readings, during service 29, 33; secular 51–2
reception, the 64–76; at home 65, 68–9; in a hotel 66, 69–71; organizing your own 75–6; sit down or buffet 67–8; food at 68–9, 70–1
register office 11, 44–7; giving notice at 25–6; wedding ceremony in 45–6; dress for 79
rings, engagement and wedding 15–17
Roman Catholic Church 10, 38–41; proportion of weddings in 10; wedding service in the 41

Scotland, marriage in 27
sex 104–5
shoes, bride's 81
speeches 53
suit, bridegroom's 85–6; cost of 89

traditions 1–2, 29–32, 64, 82–3; in proposing 5–6

veils 82
videoing the wedding 62–3; at a register office 46

wedding: ring, see rings; date 20–1; what kind of 21–4; see also legal requirements, church weddings, humanist weddings, register office weddings, abroad

Overcoming Common Problems

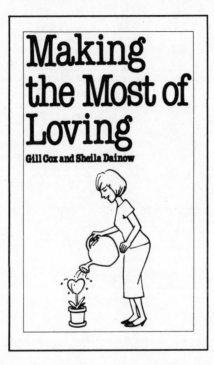

Loving is about sharing, caring, having fun, being needed and being special to someone. But all relationships have their problems. Anyone can learn to solve their problems by talking more openly and honestly, and make the most of themself and their relationships.

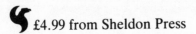 £4.99 from Sheldon Press